LEADER

W9-BTB-534

Colossians: navigating successfully through cultural chaos

Bible Study That Builds Christian Community

LifeWay | Small Groups

Colossians: Navigating Successfully Through Cultural Chaos
Leader Book
© 2004 Serendipity House
Sixth printing 2012

All rights reserved. No part of this work may be reproduced, stored in a retrieval system, or transmitted in any form or by any means, electronic or mechanical, including photocopying and recording, without express written permission of the publisher. Requests for permission should be addressed to Serendipity House, One LifeWay Plaza, Nashville, TN 37234-0152.

ISBN: 978-1-5749-4139-5
Item: 001241024

Dewey Decimal: 227.7
Subject Headings: BIBLE. N.T. COLOSSIANS--STUDY \ CHRISTIAN LIFE

Unless otherwise indicated, Scripture quotations are taken from the Holman Christian Standard Bible, © copyright 2000 by Holman Bible Publishers. Used by permission.

Scripture quotations marked (NIV) are from the Holy Bible, New International Version, copyright © 1973, 1978, 1984 by International Bible Society. Used by permission.

Scripture quotations marked (NRSV) are from the New Revised Standard Version of the Bible, copyright © 1989 by the Division of Christian Education of the National Council of Churches of Christ in the United States of America. Used by permission. All rights reserved.

Scripture quotations marked (NEB) are from The New English Bible. Copyright © Oxford University Press and Cambridge University Press, 1961, 1970. All rights reserved. Reprinted by permission.

To purchase additional copies of this resource or other studies:
ORDER ONLINE at www.SerendipityHouse.com
WRITE Serendipity House, One LifeWay Plaza, Nashville, TN 37234-0152
FAX (615) 251-5933
PHONE (800) 458-2772

www.SerendipityHouse.com
1-800-458-2772

Printed in the United States of America

Contents

Core Values

Community: The purpose of this curriculum is to build community within the body of believers around Jesus Christ.

Group Process: To build community, the curriculum must be designed to take a group through a step-by-step process of sharing your story with one another.

Interactive Bible Study: To share your "story," the approach to Scripture in the curriculum needs to be open-ended and right-brained—to "level the playing field" and encourage everyone to share.

Developmental Stages: To provide a healthy program in the life cycle of a group, the curriculum needs to offer courses on three levels of commitment:

(1) **Beginner Level**—low-level entry, high structure, to level the playing field;
(2) **Growth Level**—deeper Bible study, flexible structure, to encourage group accountability;
(3) **Discipleship Level**—in-depth Bible study, open structure, to move the group into high gear.

Target Audiences: To build community throughout the culture of the church, the curriculum needs to be flexible, adaptable, and transferable into the structure of the average church.

Mission: To expand the kingdom of God one person at a time by filling the "empty chair." (We add an extra chair to each group session to remind us of our mission.)

Group Covenant

It is important that your group covenant together, agreeing to live out important group values. Once these values are agreed upon, your group will be on its way to experiencing Christian community. It's very important that your group discuss these values—preferably as you begin this study. The first session would be most appropriate. (Check the rules to which each member of your group agrees.)

- ☐ **Priority:** While you are in this course of study, you give the group meetings priority.
- ☐ **Participation:** Everyone is encouraged to participate and no one dominates.
- ☐ **Respect:** Everyone is given the right to his or her own opinion, and all questions are encouraged and respected.
- ☐ **Confidentiality:** Anything that is said in the meeting is never repeated outside the meeting.
- ☐ **Life Change:** We will regularly assess our own life-change goals and encourage one another in our pursuit of Christlikeness.
- ☐ **Empty Chair:** The group stays open to reaching new people at every meeting.
- ☐ **Care and Support:** Permission is given to call upon each other at any time, especially in times of crisis. The group will provide care for every member.
- ☐ **Accountability:** We agree to let the members of the group hold us accountable to the commitments we make in whatever loving ways we decide upon.
- ☐ **Mission:** We will do everything in our power to start a new group.
- ☐ **Ministry:** The group will encourage one another to volunteer and serve in a ministry and to support missions by giving financially and/or personally serving.

For the Leader

Each group meeting consists of a three-part agenda:

Icebreaker – Fun questions designed to warm the group and build understanding about other group members. These questions prepare the group for meaningful discussion throughout the session.

Bible Study – The heart of each session is the Bible study time. The Life Connections series involves six easy-to-understand segments.

1. **Scripture Reading** – Each Bible study begins with the reading of the focal passage.
2. **About Today's Session** – This section of the Bible Study time is designed to peak the interest of attendees and introduce the theme for the session. In most instances there will be a reminder of what was studied the previous week, a captivating illustration or analogy related to everyday life, and a statement describing what life-changing topic will be given attention.
3. **Identifying with the Story** – During this segment of the Bible Study, subgroups learn more about each other by answering questions that will help them share their story. These questions directly relate to the topic for the day.
4. **Today's Session** – This short teaching time will be led by the Master Teacher. These scripted teachings include a depth of biblical understanding, fascinating illustrations, analogies, statistics, and stories that will spark questions and conviction.
5. **Learning from the Story** – Subgroups will gather to answer a series of questions that anticipate commitment to applying the truths taught.
6. **Life Change Lessons** – The Master Teacher gives practical suggestions that will aid attendees in carrying out the commitments they make.

Caring Time – All study should point us to action. Each session ends with prayer and direction in caring for the needs of group members. Time is also provided to pray for the "empty chair." The empty chair is a visible symbol of the need for each group to lead an unbeliever to a relationship with Jesus Christ.

The cross icon and boxed text represents portions of the student book that have been reprinted in this book.

Every Life Connections group must fill three important roles. Each responsibility is vital to the success of the class.

Teacher – The teacher is the key leader of any Life Connections group.
It is the responsibility of the teacher to:

1. enlist facilitators and apprentices.
2. make facilitators and apprentices aware of their roles and be certain these responsibilities are carried out.
3. meet periodically with facilitators to train, encourage, and inspire them.
4. cast vision for and keep the group focused on the goals of the group.
5. guide group members to understand and commit to the group covenant.
6. be sure the group utilizes, fills, and evangelizes through use of the empty chair concept.
7. act as the Master Teacher for the group.
8. keep the group on task throughout each session.

Facilitator – Each subgroup will have a facilitator.
It is the responsibility of the facilitators to:

1. lead each individual in their subgroup to participate in Icebreaker activities.
2. involve all members in their subgroup in the Identifying with the Story section of the study.
3. guide those in their subgroup to commit to apply the lessons learned in the Learning from the Story section of the weekly session.
4. with sensitivity and wisdom lead their subgroup to minister to one another during the Caring Time and involve their subgroup in ministry and evangelism.
5. minister to the needs of their subgroup members and lead them to minister to the needs of one another both during and between meetings.

Apprentice – Every subgroup must have an apprentice. When the group consistently has eight or more in attendance, the group should divide into two groups. The apprentice will become the facilitator of the new group and choose an apprentice who will someday be the facilitator of a group.
It is the role of the apprentice to:

1. learn from the facilitator of their group.
2. make welcome all new subgroup members.
3. be certain student books and pens or pencils are available for all participants.
4. turn in prayer requests.
5. encourage participation by actively participating themselves.
6. lead the group when the facilitator is unavailable.

For more information and frequently asked questions about Life Connections, visit our Web site at *www.serendipityhouse.com*.

Session 1 Outrageous Anticipation

Prepare for the Session

	READINGS	REFLECTIVE QUESTIONS
Monday	Colossians 1:1-8	What is happening in your faith or in the faith of a loved one that makes you thankful today?
Tuesday	Psalm 42:1-5	What has been bringing you down recently? How does your faith lift you back up?
Wednesday	Isaiah 40:28-31	In what way do you need God to "renew your strength" for the weeks ahead?
Thursday	Romans 5:3-5	What have you hoped in that has disappointed you? How is your hope in Christ different?
Friday	Romans 8:18-25	What signs of hope do you see in the world around you?
Saturday	1 Peter 1:3-5	To what degree is your hope built on what God has done in Jesus Christ?
Sunday	Revelation 21:1-5	How important is it to you that God will bring about "a new heaven and a new earth"? What encourages you most about this promise?

OUR GOALS FOR THIS SESSION ARE:

In groups of 6–8, gather people in a horseshoe configuration.

Make sure everyone has a name tag.

Take time to share information on class parties that are coming up as well as any relevant church events.

INTRODUCE THE ICEBREAKER ACTIVITY: The students have been given instructions in their books.

After the Icebreaker say something like, "Just like people develop a reputation, so do churches. The church at Colossae had developed a rather good one, and Paul wanted to affirm them for it. Today we will look at what that reputation was and what Paul's words to them about that reputation say to us."

Hand out the Prayer/Praise Report. A sample copy is on pages 166-167. Have people write down prayer requests and praises. Then have the prayer coordinator collect the report and make copies for use during the Caring Time.

BIBLE STUDY
- to consider the importance of personal affirmation to Christian fellowship
- to give some thought to the role of hope in relation to love and faith
- to learn about the beginning of the church at Colossae

LIFE CHANGE
- to find three new Christians to affirm in their new faith
- to testify to the hope within us
- to write a letter to ourselves affirming our own growth in the faith

Icebreaker (10-15 minutes)

A Good Reputation. Go around the group on question 1 and let everyone share. Then go around again on questions 2 and 3, as time allows.

1. By the time you were in high school, what did you have a reputation for?

☐ high academic achievement
☐ lack of achievement
☐ high athletic achievement
☐ my Christian character
☐ high musical achievement
☐ my sense of humor
☐ my rebelliousness
☐ hard work
☐ my prowess with the opposite sex
☐ the creativity I showed in getting into trouble
☐ other: ________________

2. As an adult, in what area of your life have you worked hardest at building your reputation?

☐ in my professional life
☐ in my family life
☐ in my political influence
☐ in my spiritual life
☐ in my community involvement
☐ in my character
☐ other: ________________

3. If the people who know you best were asked what you are known for today, what would they say?

LEARNING FROM THE BIBLE

COLOSSIANS 1:1-8

Have a member of the class, selected ahead of time, read Colossians 1:1-8.

Bible Study (30-45 minutes)

The Scripture for this week:

[1]Paul, an apostle of Christ Jesus by God's will, and Timothy our brother:

[2]To the saints and faithful brothers in Christ in Colossae. Grace to you and peace from God our Father.

[3]We always thank God, the Father of our Lord Jesus Christ, when we pray for you, [4]for we have heard of your faith in Christ Jesus and of the love you have for all the saints [5]because of the hope reserved for you in heaven. You have already heard about this hope in the message of truth, [6]the gospel that has come to you. It is bearing fruit and growing all over the world, just as it has among you since the day you heard it and recognized God's grace in the truth. [7]You learned this from Epaphras, our much loved fellow slave. He is a faithful minister of the Messiah on your behalf, [8]and he has told us about your love in the Spirit.

notes:

...about today's session (5 minutes)

Summarize these introductory remarks. Be sure to include the underlined information, which gives the answers to the student book questions (provided in the margin).

THE IMPORTANCE OF HOPE

When are people most likely to commit suicide?

Those who have studied suicide often report that a person commits suicide not when things are at their worst, but when they have run out of hope for things to get better. Psychologically and spiritually, hope is the most essential element of life. The most important questions of life then become, where does a person find hope and how is that hope maintained?

On what inadequate sources of hope have people sometimes relied?

Throughout history people have tried putting their hope in different places. Some have put that hope in a natural progress of humankind. In the earlier part of the Twentieth Century a popular saying was "Every day in every way, things are getting better." But then we saw the devastation caused by the nuclear arms that people invented. In terrorism, child abuse, and genocide, we have also seen the tremendous evil of which humankind is capable. Human science, rather than a source of salvation, is just as often a source of more efficient killing. Few believe so naively in natural human progress any more. Movies such as *Minority Report* express popular frustration over attempts at human-built Utopias. Others have put their hope in such mystical sources as astrology. The 60s were supposed to be "the Age of Aquarius," the age of peace and understanding. It didn't exactly work that way. Some have gone so far as to wait for rescue from some more enlightened civilization from outer space, but most agree that such actions are out of touch with reality.

What does true hope require?

True hope requires a solid source for that hope. Throughout the centuries millions have held to the hope in the message of the gospel of Jesus Christ. The Colossians to whom Paul wrote had heard of this hope and held to it. In this first session, we will be looking at what this hope meant to them.

notes:

Remain in groups of 6–8 people, in a horseshoe configuration.

In this small-group session, students will be responding to the following questions that will help them share their stories in terms of the hope that the Colossians had heard of and held to.

Have the students explore these questions together.

Identifying with the Story (5-7 minutes)

1. Who is someone you thank God for when you pray? What characteristic does this person have that you especially appreciate?

2. Who, above everyone else, is most responsible for you hearing and understanding the hope of the gospel of Jesus Christ? What did this person say or do that influenced you?

3. When it comes to thanking others for what they have done or are doing, how do you show your appreciation?

- ☐ send them a thank you note or personal letter
- ☐ pull them aside and tell them face-to-face
- ☐ do something for them to show my thanks
- ☐ do nothing, and just assume they know
- ☐ remind them of what they *have not* done—I don't want them to rest on their laurels!
- ☐ other: ____________________

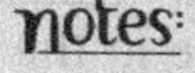

today's session (15-20 minutes)

Share with your class the following information which you may modify according to your own perspectives and teaching needs. The answers to the student book questions (provided in the margin) are underlined.

Who established the church at Colossae? What seems to have been the nature of Paul's relationship to this church?

What did Paul thank God for in this church?

What two tools do people use to influence others? Which approach did Paul almost always use first in his letters?

Paul most frequently wrote to churches that he established in order to encourage them and help them face various challenges. This was one way he nurtured the life he had been instrumental in starting. However, the church at Colossae was not one he established, as seems evident from verse 7 of our text for today: "You learned this [the gospel] from Epaphras, our much loved fellow slave." In fact, he had never even personally encountered these Christians at Colossae (2:1). Why then did he feel the need to write to them? The most likely explanation is that Paul had won Epaphras to the faith and had deputized him to evangelize certain areas including the Lycus valley where Colossae was located. Thus, while these converts were not Paul's "children" in the faith, he would have seen them as his "grandchildren" through Epaphras. He would have had the great desire–and authority–to guide and support these spiritual grandchildren.

Affirming the Positive in People

Paul began his letter to the Colossians as he did most of his other letters: after a greeting he thanked God for them and pointed out their accomplishments in the Lord. Here in Colossians, specifically, he thanked them for the faith and love they had. These had sprung from the hope they had in Jesus Christ. Such a positive beginning is typical of Paul's letters (only Galatians, where Paul was very angry with the church for its legalism, breaks the pattern). People typically used two tools for influencing others: discouraging negative behavior through punishment and rebuke, and encouraging positive behavior through affirmation and praise. Paul certainly at times used the first approach (see, for instance, 2 Corinthians 11:1-15; Galatians 1:6-10), but his pattern was to begin with encouraging the positive behaviors he found in his readers. Significantly, this is in line with current approaches to childcare. Child psychologists and educators most often agree that it is more effective to affirm the positive behavior in our children than to punish the negative (although such punishment may sometimes be necessary.) Paul thought of his readers as his children and (in this case) grandchildren, and he sought to lead them first of all through positive affirmation. He did so in spite of the fact that he did have some concerns about them. Specifically, he was concerned that they were being led astray by a strange philosophy based on human traditions (2:8) and involving the worship of angels (2:18.) As serious as such a heresy might have been, he still led with the positive and affirmed what they were doing right.

Paul here affirmed his readers' faith and love, which came out of their hope. Interestingly enough, you have here the three great virtues that

today's session (cont'd)

Paul affirms in 1 Corinthians 13. While in that chapter Paul states that "the greatest of these is love," here he says that his readers' faith and love come out of their *hope*. How does faith and love come out of hope? The NIV says that they *"spring from* the hope that is stored up for you in heaven" (1:5). This hope that is stored up or "reserved" (Holman) for us is a hope that death will not defeat us and that life will be eternal in Jesus Christ. Such a hope has several implications for our "faith in Christ Jesus" and "love for all the saints."

A Love That Grows Out of Hope

In what two ways does our Christian hope intensify the love we have for fellow Christians?

Looking first at the effect of eternal hope on our love for others, love is more secure when we have the hope that it is forever. It is hard to fully love that which you know you will soon lose. People tend to hold on less tightly when they know that permanent separation is inevitable. When our hope promises that our relationships in Jesus Christ are forever, we are free to fully treasure them. Christ told us, "Don't collect for yourselves treasures on earth, where moth and rust destroy and where thieves break in and steal. But collect for yourselves treasures in heaven, where neither moth nor rust destroys, and where thieves don't break in and steal" (Matt. 6:19-20). In Christ, our love relationships are part of our eternal treasure. Even if those relationships are interrupted by death, we know that we will be able to enjoy them eternally. First Thessalonians 4:13-14 assures us, "We do not want you to be uninformed, brothers, concerning those who are asleep, so that you will not grieve like the rest, who have no hope. Since we believe that Jesus died and rose again, in the same way God will bring with Him those who have fallen asleep through Jesus." In Christ, we never really have to say "good-bye" – it is always, "see you later!"

Our hope in Christ also intensifies our love by uniting us with the bond of this hope. Love becomes more intense when you share a common vision of where you are going. Sports teams are bound to each other by their passion to win a championship. The cast of a play is bound together by their passion to have a successful production that speaks to the heart of the audience. And in the same way Christians are bound together by their common hope in Jesus Christ.

A Fuller Faith Through Hope

Our hope also feeds our faith in Christ. Certainly our faith in Christ is important for this life. It helps to bring meaning and abundance to this life. However, without our hope in something more to come, that faith would not be all that it can be. Paul points this out in 1 Corinthians 15:13-14: "But if there is no resurrection of the dead, then Christ has

Where else in his letters did Paul speak of the importance of Christian hope to faith?

not been raised; and if Christ has not been raised, then our preaching is without foundation, and so is your faith." He adds in verses 17-19, "And if Christ has not been raised, your faith is worthless; you are still in your sins. Therefore those who have fallen asleep in Christ have also perished. If we have placed our hope in Christ for this life only, we should be pitied more than anyone." So it is clear that faith and hope are inextricably intertwined, and that is why it can be said that faith "springs from" (NIV) the hope we have within us.

While Paul here presents faith and love coming from hope, we should not conclude from this that he is recanting what he said in 1 Corinthians that "the greatest of these is love." Love is the clearest sign of God's presence (1 John 4:12.) However, here we learn another aspect of the truth. Christian hope has a vital role in generating and maintaining that love, as well as the faith which lifts us up.

notes:

Remain in groups of 6–8 people, in a horseshoe configuration.

In this small-group session, students will be applying the lessons of the text to their own lives through the following questions.

The students were asked (in the student book) to choose an answer for each question and explain why.

Learning from the Story (5-7 minutes)

1. If someone told you that they had heard of "the love your church has for all the saints," what would be your reaction?
   - ☐ They obviously have not been to our board meetings.
   - ☐ The saints, maybe, but we have a hard time loving those sinners.
   - ☐ The love is real—but we need to work on our faith more.
   - ☐ I would not be surprised—the love is what brought me here.
2. In what way has the hope you have heard and learned about in the gospel born fruit (had visible results) in your life?
3. Where do you see the gospel growing and spreading today? In what way do you feel called to help the good news of Christ grow?

notes:

Share with the class the following thoughts on how the lessons of this text might be applied today. The answers to the student book questions (provided in the margin) are underlined unless the question requires a personal answer.

In what two ways have Christian leaders sometimes emphasized the negative over the positive?

What is often the result of trying to motivate people by such a negative approach?

life change lessons (5-7 minutes)

In this study we have seen two positive factors which led to the growth of the gospel: (1) the affirmation of leaders like Paul who tried to see first the positive things that were happening in the lives of converts; and (2) the hope of the gospel which pulled people forward. Sometimes Christian leaders in other eras have emphasized the negative over the positive. Instead of leading people by the hope God gives, they have sought to push them by fear of punishment. Instead of affirming the progress people make, they continually pointed out the areas where the persons fail. By so doing they, consciously or unconsciously, have sought to pull guilt strings. The result of this kind of manipulation is most often despair and resignation to spiritual failure.

In applying today's lesson, then, we need to take an approach that holds fast to the positive approach of Paul. Specifically, we should:

1. FIND THREE NEW CHRISTIANS TO AFFIRM. These can be youth or adults who have been recently baptized or come forward to declare a decision for Christ. Talk to them face-to-face, or give them a call. Affirm first of all their decision to come to Christ. Then look for other things they are doing to make this life change real – participating in a Sunday School class, taking notes on the sermon, asking questions in order to learn. Don't give unsolicited advice. Rather take every opportunity to affirm their positive steps.

2. TESTIFY TO THE HOPE WITHIN YOU. Find at least one person you can tell about your Christian hope. This should not be academic! Share what excites you about what Christ has done for you and the promise of hope that is before you.

3. WRITE A LETTER TO YOURSELF. Pretend that you are Paul writing to yourself. Affirm what Paul might affirm about your faith and hope, and the "fruit" your life is bearing.

notes:

CARING TIME
Remain in groups of 6–8 people, in a horseshoe configuration.

Hand out the Prayer/ Praise Report to the entire group. Ask each subgroup to pray for the empty chair. Pray specifically for God to guide you to someone to bring next week to fill that chair.

After a sufficient time of prayer in subgroups, close in a corporate prayer. Say, "Next week we will talk about: 'Just Do It.' "

Remind participants of the daily Scripture readings and reflective questions found on page 20.

Caring Time (15-20 minutes)

This is the time for developing and expressing your caring for each other. Begin by having group members finish this sentence:

"The hope I have for what will happen in this class in the weeks to come is ..."

Pray for these hopes, as well as the concerns that are listed on the Prayer/Praise Report. Include prayer for the empty chair, and ask God to guide you to someone to invite for next week.

If you would like to pray silently, say "Amen" when you have finished your prayer, so that the next person will know when to start.

notes:

BIBLE STUDY NOTES

Reference Notes

Use these notes to gain further understanding of the text as you study on your own:

COLOSSIANS 1:2

saints. This term is not used in the Roman Catholic sense of those elevated officially to a special status by the church, or in the popular sense of people with morally flawless behavior. Rather the "saints" are all persons sanctified or made holy by the blood of Jesus Christ.

COLOSSIANS 1:2 (cont'd)

Colossae. This city lay about 100 miles east of Ephesus in the Lycus River Valley. Since it was located on a major trade route from Ephesus, Colossae was considered a great city in the days of Xerxes, the Persian king (fifth century B.C.). One hundred years later, it had developed into a prosperous commercial center on account of its weaving industry. By the time of Paul, Colossae's prominence had diminished though its sister cities, Laodicea and Hierapolis, were still prospering.

Grace to you and peace. This is a Christianized adaptation of a common greeting. This letter highlights the reality of God's grace through Christ and the reconciliation (peace) that results.

COLOSSIANS 1:4–5

faith...love...hope. This triad of Christian graces is arranged and expanded upon in various ways throughout the New Testament (Rom. 5:1-5; 1 Cor. 13:13; Gal. 5:5-6; Eph. 4:2-5; 1 Thess. 1:3,5:8; Heb. 6:10-12; 1 Pet. 1:3-8). The center of the Christian faith is Jesus Christ; the essence of its lifestyle is love; and the sure hope of a future with Christ is its motivation.

COLOSSIANS 1:6

bearing fruit. See Mark 4:1-20,26-29.

growing all over the world. Within 30 years after Jesus' resurrection, the gospel had spread from Palestine throughout the Roman Empire.

heard it and recognized God's grace in the truth. The words *all* or *everything* appear repeatedly in 1:1-23. Through this emphasis, Paul is countering the false teachers' claims that there is more to learn and experience about life with God than what can be found in the message of God's grace in Christ (2:4,8).

COLOSSIANS 1:7

Epaphras. A native Colossian who established the church there and worked for Christ throughout the Lycus valley (4:12; Philem. 23).

notes:

Session

2

Just Do It

Prepare for the Session

	READINGS	REFLECTIVE QUESTIONS
Monday	Colossians 1:9-10	What do you need to do today to "walk worthy of the Lord"?
Tuesday	Colossians 1:11-12	In what situation will you especially need patience in the coming week?
Wednesday	Colossians 1:13-14	Where do you see a "domain of darkness" in the world around you? In what way(s) have you been part of that darkness?
Thursday	Acts 26:19-20	How has your repentance for past wrongs been reflected in your behavior? What can you do today to demonstrate that repentance is real?
Friday	Galatians 5:22-26	Which fruit of the Spirit are you best manifesting in your life? Which fruit do you need to work on, with the Holy Spirit's help?
Saturday	1 John 3:10*b*-15	Who are you having difficulty loving right now? What could help you change your attitude toward this-person?
Sunday	1 John 5:3-5	Which of God's commandments have you found burdensome? How could obedience to that commandment help you "conquer the world"?

OUR GOALS FOR THIS SESSION ARE:

In groups of 6–8, gather people in a horseshoe configuration.

Make sure everyone has a name tag.

Take time to share information on class parties that are coming up as well as any relevant church events.

INTRODUCE THE ICEBREAKER ACTIVITY: The students have been given instructions in their books.

After the Icebreaker say something like, "Being whisked away from our troubles into a magical kingdom can be more than a fantasy: our Scripture for today says that it is in truth what Christ will in some sense do for all of His followers. However, we are also called to live a life worthy of the One who does this for us. In our session today we will look at what this means."

Hand out the Prayer/Praise Report. A sample copy is on pages 166-167. Have people write down prayer requests and praises. Then have the prayer coordinator collect the report and make copies for use during the Caring Time.

BIBLE STUDY
- to understand that we are called to live in a manner worthy of our Lord Jesus Christ
- to see how living in a manner worthy of Christ requires help and strength from God
- to consider what it means for a Christian life to "bear fruit"

LIFE CHANGE
- to pray daily for the other members of this group and their growth
- to pray for our own spiritual strengthening
- to find one new way to put our faith into action

Icebreaker (10-15 minutes)

Rescue Operation. Go around the group on question 1 and let everyone share. Then go around again on questions 2 and 3, as time allows.

1. When you were in grade school, from what or whom did you most feel the need to be rescued?

   ☐ the demands of my parents
   ☐ a pesky sibling
   ☐ the opposite sex
   ☐ school work
   ☐ the neighborhood bully
   ☐ work of any kind
   ☐ my own shyness
   ☐ other: ______________

2. As an adult, from what or whom do you most feel the need to be rescued?

   ☐ telemarketers and solicitors
   ☐ demanding family members
   ☐ my addiction to sweets and junk food
   ☐ the scary world we live in
   ☐ bills
   ☐ my own bad decisions
   ☐ other: ______________________

3. If you could be whisked off to a magical kingdom, what would be the most important qualities you would want that kingdom to have?

notes:

LEARNING FROM THE BIBLE

COLOSSIANS 1:9-14

Have a member of the class, selected ahead of time, read Colossians 1:9-14.

Bible Study (30-45 minutes)

The Scripture for this week:

9For this reason also, since the day we heard this, we haven't stopped praying for you. We are asking that you may be filled with the knowledge of His will in all wisdom and spiritual understanding, 10so that you may walk worthy of the Lord, fully pleasing to Him, bearing fruit in every good work and growing in the knowledge of God. 11May you be strengthened with all power, according to His glorious might, for all endurance and patience, with joy 12giving thanks to the Father, who has enabled you to share in the saints' inheritance in the light. 13He has rescued us from the domain of darkness and transferred us into the kingdom of the Son He loves, 14in whom we have redemption, the forgiveness of sins.

notes:

Summarize these introductory remarks. Be sure to include the underlined information, which gives the answers to the student book questions (provided in the margin).

...about today's session (5 minutes)

THE CHRISTIAN LIFE

What have Christians down through the ages discovered to be impossible?

Some people believe and teach that living a good life is the way a person can "earn" his or her way into heaven. But Christians down through the ages have discovered the impossibility of such an approach. No matter how hard we try, moral failures build up. It was this realization that led Martin Luther to initiate the Protestant Reformation. People rediscovered biblical teachings like Ephesians 2:8-9, "For by grace you are saved through faith, and this is not from yourselves; it is God's gift—not from works, so that no one can boast."

Why are we to do good works?

However, since works are not the basis of our salvation, some people make the mistake of assuming that good works are unimportant. Nothing could be further from the truth. Ephesians 2:8-9 is followed up by this statement in verse 10: "For we are His creation—created in Christ Jesus for good works, which God prepared ahead of time so that we should walk in them." And here in Colossians we receive the challenge that we are to "walk worthy of the Lord, fully pleasing [to Him], bearing fruit in every good work and growing in the knowledge of God." The idea then is that we are not doing good works in order to earn God's favor or our own salvation, but to say thank you to God for His free gift of grace. Because we have learned the wonders of God's love and grace in Jesus Christ, we turn our lives over to Him and seek to emulate His love and grace in our own lives. It's like when we were children many of us were told not to do anything that reflected poorly on the family. By God's grace we are part of His family, and our actions should show to all that we are part of a family of love and righteousness. In this session, we will be delving into a deeper understanding of what it means to walk in a way that is worthy of our Lord in this manner.

What characteristics describe the family of God?

2

notes:

Remain in groups of 6–8 people, in a horseshoe configuration.

In this small-group session, students will be responding to the following questions that will help them share their stories in terms of the challenges of Colossians 1:9-14.

Have the students explore these questions together.

Identifying with the Story (5-7 minutes)

1. When you were in grade school, whom did you most want to please by your behavior? Do you remember a time when you did something to disappoint this person? How did you feel, and what did you do?

2. When do you remember receiving an honor that you felt unworthy to receive? What did you do in response?

3. In general, which of the following responses best reflects how worthy you feel of the good things that have happened to you?
   - ☐ "What good things?"
   - ☐ "What have I ever done to deserve even one of the pleasures I've known?"
   - ☐ "Hey, I am as worthy as the next person!"
   - ☐ "Basically, I've earned what I've gotten in life."
   - ☐ "I deserve much better than I'm getting!"

notes:

Share with your class the following information which you may modify according to your own perspectives and teaching needs. The answers to the student book questions (provided in the margin) are underlined.

today's session (15-20 minutes)

2

When people who are non-Christians look at Christians they do not see directly what they believe: they see what those Christians *do*. That is why what we do is especially important. It is a witness to the kind of Lord we serve. Yet, since we are all imperfect, our witness will always be imperfect. What then should we do? This passage from Colossians is a good guide. It tells us *why* we should walk in a way worthy of the Lord, *how* we can do the best job of walking in that manner, and *what it means* to walk worthy of the Lord. Let's look at all three of these topics.

Why We Should Walk Worthy

What are two reasons we should walk in a manner worthy of our Lord?

Why we should walk worthy of the Lord is the "bottom line" of it all, and significantly the explanation of why is the last (bottom!) line of this passage: "He has rescued us from the domain of darkness and transferred us into the kingdom of the Son He loves, in whom we have redemption, the forgiveness of sins." We should walk worthy of the Lord <u>because of all He has done for us, specifically, saving us from our sin and making it possible for us to be part of the eternal fellowship of His kingdom.</u> When we fully realize all that means, we can be nothing but thankful. Death no longer has dominion over us! The relationships which add so richly to this life do not have to end if we are in the fellowship of Christ. The way we live our lives is our "thank you note" to God for all He has done.

We should, however, also point out that part of the reason we seek to live in this way is that what God has saved us out of really is a life of darkness: "He has rescued us from the domain of darkness." What does that mean? People who are in darkness for a long time get used to it and they think it is somewhat normal. If you come into a darkened room and turn on the light, people will wince and scowl at you, and probably ask you to turn it off. Their eyes are used to the darkness. John speaks much of this theme of darkness and light in his Gospel. He writes in John 3:19-21: "This, then, is the judgment: the light has come into the world, and people loved darkness rather than the light because their deeds were evil. For everyone who practices wicked things hates the light and avoids it, so that his deeds may not be exposed. But anyone who lives by the truth comes to the light, so that his works may be shown to be accomplished by God." While there is a natural reason to avoid light sometimes (the need for eyes to rest), spiritually, avoiding the light and dwelling in the darkness detracts from life. In the darkness a person runs into things, and they are deprived of the richness of the color of the

today's session (cont'd)

world around them. In the same way spiritual darkness detracts from the richness of life, takes away our sense of direction and even enslaves us. And so we should walk in the way God calls us to avoid falling back into the slavery of "the domain of darkness." Paul says it this way in Romans 6:16-18: "Do you not know that if you offer yourselves to someone as obedient slaves, you are slaves of that one you obey—either of sin leading to death or of obedience leading to righteousness? But thank God that, although you used to be slaves of sin, you obeyed from the heart that pattern of teaching you were entrusted to, and having been liberated from sin, you became enslaved to righteousness."

What are two qualities of a life of sin that should make us want to avoid that life?

People who have acknowledged an addiction, whether that be an addiction to drugs or alcohol, an addiction to tobacco, or a more socially acceptable addiction like overeating, know what it can mean to be enslaved to something that is destroying them. But what we sometimes don't realize is that all sin is both addictive and destructive in this way. It is a domain of darkness, and to walk worthy of the Lord is to walk away from it.

How We can Walk Worthy

What are two ways that God helps us to walk worthy of Him?

To say we have reasons why we should walk worthy does not necessarily mean we can do so. We have already noted that we are all human beings who are prone to sin. On our own strength we have great difficulty walking in a manner worthy of the Lord. But Paul writes some things to the Colossians which encourage us in this matter. He writes in verses 9-10, "We are asking that you may be filled with the knowledge of His will in all wisdom and spiritual understanding, so that you may walk worthy of the Lord." God helps us walk worthy of Him. Specifically, we see here that He helps us by giving us *direction*. On our own, we are all prone to taking wrong turns, to losing our direction. But God fills us with His wisdom and understanding *so that* we may walk worthy of the Lord. Of course, for this to help us we have to be receptive to this kind of direction, and that comes through opening ourselves through prayer.

Paul doesn't just pray for this direction to help the Colossians. He also prays for another kind of aid that will help them walk worthy of the Lord, and he writes of this in verse 11: "May you be strengthened with all power, according to His glorious might, for all endurance and patience." To know God's direction without receiving God's *strength*, is like having a map for a trip, but being without provisions. God supplies us with both map and provisions.

What It Means to Walk Worthy

What are the two main elements of walking worthy of the Lord?

Finally, it is important that we see in more concrete terms what it means to walk in a manner worthy of our Lord. The key is in verse 10: "bearing fruit in every good work and growing in the knowledge of God." So there are two elements in walking worthy: the outer element of producing good works, and the inner element of spiritual growth.

Let's look first at the element of spiritual growth. This means that walking worthy includes the spiritual disciplines that help us grow in Christ: attending worship services, being involved in personal and corporate study of Scripture, as well as regular reliance on prayer, silence, and devotional reading. Attendance at worship helps us to develop a support system for our growing, as well as giving us regular guidance from spiritual leaders. Scriptural and devotional study help us know more about God and God's will for our lives. Scriptural study in particular helps us know God's Word and how God has revealed Himself to us through time. Prayer makes the connection more personal. For a person to "grow in the knowledge of God," prayer has to be more than something we do as an escape once we get in trouble. It has to be a regular discipline, like physical exercise. Doctors tell us that there is nothing worse for a person's heart than to go out and do vigorous exercise once in a blue moon when the body isn't used to it. Conditioning comes from *regular* exercise, and that is true with prayer as well. Our prayer time should also include time for silence. Psalm 46:10 tells us, "Be still, and know that I am God" (NIV). Such quiet time not only helps us get in touch with God, but it also helps us get in touch with ourselves. Both are important to growing in the knowledge of God. To know ourselves is to know the purpose for which God made us, and knowing that purpose helps us know Him better.

To truly walk in a manner worthy of our Lord, however, we have do more than learn: we have to use what we learn in action. We have to do works that glorify God, and that means imitating Jesus Christ. The Apostle John emphasizes this a great deal in both his Gospel and his letters. Jesus says in John 14:12, "I assure you: The one who believes in Me will also do the works that I do. And he will do even greater works than these, because I am going to the Father." And in 1 John 2:6, we read, "The one who says he remains in Him should walk just as He walked." This means showing love to each other: "This is how we have come to know love: He laid down His life for us. We should also lay down our lives for our brothers" (1 John 3:16.)

What is the essence of what it means to walk in a manner worthy of our Lord?

Loving in the spirit of Christ is then the essence of what it means to walk in a manner worthy of the Lord. It is that lifestyle to which we should aspire.

Remain in groups of 6–8 people, in a horseshoe configuration.

In this small-group session, students will be applying the lessons of the text to their own lives through the following questions.

The students were asked (in the student book) to choose an answer for each question and explain why.

Learning from the Story (5-7 minutes)

1. Looking back at your life right now, when would you say you were most part of a "domain of darkness" (v. 13)? How did Christ rescue you from that time?

2. Where do you feel you are right now in terms of "growing in the knowledge of God" (v. 10)?
   - ▢ I am a tiny sprig of life, freshly emerged from the ground.
   - ▢ I am a little seedling, still tender and vulnerable, but growing fast.
   - ▢ I am a strong, healthy tree, bearing fruit.
   - ▢ I am a diseased tree, alive but struggling to go on.
   - ▢ I am like a giant Sequoia with firm and ancient roots.

3. What do you most need to continue to grow in the Lord?
   - ▢ more knowledge of God and the Bible
   - ▢ more affirmation and encouragement from others in the church
   - ▢ more opportunities to serve God in meaningful ways
   - ▢ more opportunities to explore my questions
   - ▢ more discipline in my prayer and devotional life
   - ▢ other: ____________________________

notes:

Share with the class the following thoughts on how the lessons of this text might be applied today. The answers to the student book questions (provided in the margin) are underlined unless the question requires a personal answer.

What do you acknowledge when you pray for strength and direction?

If you were truly to pray as Paul teaches in our Scripture for today, how would it change your prayer life?

life change lessons (5-7 minutes)

The life changes implied by this passage begin with where the passage begins: Paul praying for the Colossians. If to truly live a life worthy of the Lord we need God's strength and direction, then we need to be in prayer for that strength and direction, both praying for each other and praying for ourselves. Such prayer acknowledges that we cannot do it alone. It claims the promise made by Christ, "Keep asking, and it will be given to you. Keep searching, and you will find. Keep knocking, and the door will be opened to you" (Matt.. 7:7.)

True life change, however, must also come from an acknowledgement that the Christian life must result in "fruit," in actions of service for our Lord. Some Christians have taken the doctrine of grace to such an extreme that they have discounted works altogether. Any challenge to actually *do* something is met with the refrain, "But I am saved by grace, not works!" Such a perspective is a self-focused perversion of the gospel, and decidedly unbiblical. Our passage for today is clear that we are called to live a life worthy of the Lord, and that such a life must include "fruit" or works of service (v.10). In applying today's lesson, then, we should:

1. PRAY DAILY FOR THE OTHER MEMBERS OF THIS GROUP AND THEIR GROWTH. We pray for each other at the end of the session, but does it end there? We have talked about where we are in our spiritual growth and what our challenges are. We must remember what people have shared and pray for them. If daily prayer has not been your habit, make a goal of maintaining such a discipline for the course of this study.

2. PRAY FOR YOUR OWN SPIRITUAL STRENGTHENING. Include what Paul prayed for, for knowledge of God's will and for strength to meet the challenges you face.

3. FIND ONE NEW WAY TO PUT YOUR FAITH INTO ACTION. This can be anything from encouraging a family member to volunteering at a ministry that provides food for the needy. Shoot for something that strengthens an area of your life (family, community witness, church involvement) which you have neglected.

notes:

CARING TIME
Remain in groups of 6–8 people, in a horseshoe configuration.

Hand out the Prayer/ Praise Report to the entire group. Ask each subgroup to pray for the empty chair. Pray specifically for God to guide you to someone to bring next week to fill that chair.

After a sufficient time of prayer in subgroups, close in a corporate prayer. Say, "Next week we will talk about: 'Radical Reconciliation.'"

Remind participants of the daily Scripture readings and reflective questions found on page 32.

Caring Time (15-20 minutes)

Begin this prayer time by thanking God for rescuing us from the "domain of darkness" and transferring us into the "kingdom of the Son He loves" (v. 13). Take turns praying for each other, asking God for the strength to "walk worthy of the Lord" and direction to live according to His will. Also, use the Prayer/Praise Report and pray for the concerns listed.

Close by praying specifically for God to guide you to someone to invite for next week to fill the empty chair.

notes:

BIBLE STUDY NOTES

Reference Notes

Use these notes to gain further understanding of the text as you study on your own.

COLOSSIANS 1:9

knowledge/all wisdom and spiritual understanding. The false teachers (combining elements of Christianity, Greek mystery religions, and Judaism) defined salvation in terms of secret, divine knowledge and ecstatic experiences that could only be gained by following their regimen of ascetic disciplines and ceremonies.

COLOSSIANS 1:10

walk worthy of the Lord. Rather than esoteric knowledge and experiences, true spirituality is seen in a lifestyle that reflects the love and holiness of Jesus. ***bearing fruit.*** Scripture is consistent in insisting that the Christian life should bear fruit in works of righteousness. Jesus condemned the fig tree that bore no fruit (Matt. 21:18-22) and praised the soil that bore much produce (Matt. 13:8). Paul detailed the fruit that should be present in a life led by the Spirit: love, joy, peace, patience, kindness, goodness, faithfulness, gentleness, and self-control (Gal. 5:22-23).

COLOSSIANS 1:12

enabled. In the mystery religions, a person supposedly qualified to share in the divine through practicing various rites and disciplines (2:18). By contrast, God fully "enables" the believer to inherit His kingdom through Christ's work. ***the saints' inheritance in the light.*** Other contemporary writings show that this refers to God's angels. Through God's grace, Christians share the heavenly portion enjoyed by the angels, a point denied by the false teachers.

COLOSSIANS 1:13

the domain of darkness. Darkness is an appropriate image for the influence of the hostile spiritual forces (v. 16), since their domination only leads to spiritual and moral blindness (Luke 22:53; John 1:5; Eph. 5:8-14).

COLOSSIANS 1:14

redemption. The believers' rescue from the domain of darkness came because Jesus broke its power by His sacrificial death (v. 20; Eph. 1:7).

notes:

Session
3 Radical Reconciliation

Prepare for the Session

	READINGS	REFLECTIVE QUESTIONS
Monday	Colossians 1:15-16	What do you see in creation that especially reflects Christ?
Tuesday	Colossians 1:17-18	Is your church allowing Christ to be its true head? When have you usurped Christ's place by trying to control the church yourself?
Wednesday	Colossians 1:19-20	Imagine a completely harmonious and unified creation. How can Christ use you to accomplish this unity?
Thursday	Colossians 1:21-23	What does it mean to you to be "faultless" and "blameless"? Are you letting Christ take away your guilt, or are you holding on to it?
Friday	Romans 8:28-29	In what way, if any, are you more like Christ today than you were five years ago?
Saturday	2 Corinthians 5:17	What aspects of your old, pre-Christ self keep wanting to make a come-back? How does Christ help you claim a victory for a "new you"?
Sunday	Isaiah 11:6-9	What role does knowing God play in harmonious creation? What does this say to you about today's ecological questions?

OUR GOALS FOR THIS SESSION ARE:

In groups of 6–8, gather people in a horseshoe configuration.

Make sure everyone has a name tag.

Take time to share information on class parties that are coming up as well as any relevant church events.

INTRODUCE THE ICEBREAKER ACTIVITY: The students have been given instructions in their books.

After the Icebreaker say something like, "Most of us have something other than God that we center our lives around, at one point or another. However, for each of us there comes a time when we need to face Christ's claim to 'have first place in everything.' In this session we will take a hard look at this claim, and what our response should be."

Hand out the Prayer/Praise Report. A sample copy is on pages 166-167. Have people write down prayer requests and praises. Then have the prayer coordinator collect the report and make copies for use during the Caring Time.

BIBLE STUDY
- to gain an understanding of Christ's role as the Creator
- to consider God's plan to redeem all of creation
- to see how our own reconciliation to God fits in with God's overall plan of redemption

LIFE CHANGE
- to make sure we are personally right with God
- to act this week to find reconciliation with one other person
- to become involved in a ministry of reconciliation

Icebreaker (10-15 minutes)

The Center of My Life. Go around the group on question 1 and let everyone share. Then go around again on questions 2 and 3, as time allows.

1. What was the center of your life during the various periods of your life? For each of the categories below, mark "G" if it was the center of your life in grade school, "J" if it was the center of your life in junior high, "H" if it was the center of your life in high school, "YA" if it was the center of your life in your young adult years, and "N" if it is the center of your life now.

    ____ friends or being popular
    ____ sports or physical achievements
    ____ music, drama, or artistic achievements
    ____ business or professional achievements
    ____ family
    ____ money and possessions
    ____ pets or animals
    ____ the outdoors/exploring the natural world
    ____ faith or church gatherings
    ____ television, movies, or fictional reading
    ____ other: ______________________________

2. Pick one period of your life and share one way you expressed to others what was at the center of your life (by what you wore, the meetings you went to, what you talked about, etc.)

Icebreaker (cont'd)

3. Who shared your passion for the central interest you talked about in the above questions?

notes:

LEARNING FROM THE BIBLE

COLOSSIANS 1:15-23

Have a member of the class, selected ahead of time, read Colossians 1:15-23.

Bible Study (30-45 minutes)

The Scripture for this week:

15He is the image of the invisible God,
the firstborn over all creation;
16because by Him everything was created,
in heaven and on earth, the visible and the invisible,
whether thrones or dominions or rulers or authorities—
all things have been created through Him and for Him.
17He is before all things, and by Him all things hold together.
18He is also the head of the body, the church;
He is the beginning, the firstborn from the dead,
so that He might come to have first place in everything.
19For God was pleased to have all His fullness dwell in Him,
20and through Him to reconcile everything to Himself
by making peace through the blood of His cross —
whether things on earth or things in heaven.

21And you were once alienated and hostile in mind because of your evil actions. 22But now He has reconciled you by His physical body through His death, to present you holy, faultless, and blameless before Him— 23if indeed you remain grounded and steadfast in the faith, and are not shifted away from the hope of the gospel that you heard. This gospel has been proclaimed in all creation under heaven, and I, Paul, have become a minister of it.

...about today's session (5 minutes)

Summarize these introductory remarks. Be sure to include the underlined information, which gives the answers to the student book questions (provided in the margin).

What are some evidences of the disharmony between people and our environment? What are some examples you can think of in addition to those listed?

What are some factors that divide us? Are there any others you can think of in addition to those referred to here?

What are three aspects of reconciliation in which God wants us to be involved?

A WORLD IN DISHARMONY

All around us today we see evidence of a world in disharmony. Humanity is seemingly at war with our environment. The ozone has been depleted, our fresh water lakes and rivers have been polluted, and our forests, upon which we depend for many products and the replenishing of oxygen, are dwindling. People are also at war with each other throughout the planet, including the Middle East, North and South Korea, Ireland, Liberia, India and Pakistan. The list changes slightly from time to time, but the reality of war does not. Going one step further, this disharmony eats into our culture. We are divided by racial suspicion and hostility, by gender differences that leave the sexes distrustful toward each other, and by political differences that on some issues threaten to tear the country apart. In the midst of this disharmony, is there any hope for something better in the future? Is there anything or anyone who can bring us together? We have tried the League of Nations, the United Nations, and various human laws, treaties, and organizations; but nothing seems to do the trick. This passage from Colossians, however, points us in a more positive direction. Paul boldly proclaimed that God is going to "reconcile everything to Himself through Him by making peace by the blood of His Cross" (v. 20). Notice that it does not just say *all people*, but *everything*. God is a God of reconciliation who wants the world He created in perfection to be returned to harmony.

If God is indeed a God of reconciliation, then He wants us to be people of reconciliation. He wants us to reconcile people to each other. He wants us to reconcile people to the world in which we live. And He wants us to reconcile people to Him. Walking worthy of the Lord, which we looked at in last week's session, therefore includes being people of reconciliation so we can testify to a God of reconciliation.

In today's session we will consider what it means that Christ brings us together—reconciles us—by the blood of His cross, and we will also look at what this implies for us and our discipleship.

notes:

3

Remain in groups of 6–8 people, in a horseshoe configuration.

In this small-group session, students will be responding to the following questions that will help them share their stories in terms of the reconciliation that is the theme of this passage in Colossians.

Have the students explore these questions together.

Identifying with the Story (5-7 minutes)

1. From whom do you feel most alienated at this moment of your life?

   - ☐ a person with whom I work
   - ☐ society in general
   - ☐ the government
   - ☐ my spouse or ex-spouse
   - ☐ my parents
   - ☐ a sibling
   - ☐ my children
   - ☐ other: ________

2. If you could gauge the sense of harmony you feel with your world right now, where would it be on the following scale?

   1 · · · 2 · · · 3 · · · 4 · · · 5 · · · 6 · · · 7 · · · 8 · · · 9 · · · 10

   totally in harmony, like the best barbershop quartet — totally in discord, like a classical pianist in a heavy metal band

3. In order to feel more in harmony with the world in which you live, what do you need most?

   - ☐ a whole different world in which to live
   - ☐ a more positive perspective
   - ☐ a willingness to temper my idealism
   - ☐ a vision of where God is taking this world
   - ☐ an ability to love people as they are

notes:

today's session (15-20 minutes)

Share with your class the following information which you may modify according to your own perspectives and teaching needs. The answers to the student book questions (provided in the margin) are underlined.

What word do we use for all of the created order that implies it is a unity?

What happened that made people less than what they were created to be—the image of God?

The appeal of working with a puzzle is seeing how it all fits together in the end. In many respects that is what life itself is about. Some people feel it never does fit together. Shakespeare had a character say that life was "full of sound and fury, signifying nothing." Still, many of us have not surrendered this drive to solve the puzzle. We still want to see "the big picture." Scientists search today for what they call a "unification theory," a theory that will in one simple way explain how all of existence functions. Indeed, the word we use for all of physical reality, *universe*, implies that there is a basic unity and that everything "turns as one." The Hindu faith also proclaims that all of life has a basic unity, and they identify this unity with God. Many people who feel a kinship with life beyond the human world are drawn by such perspectives, seeing in them a rationale for dealing more responsibly with our ecology. What does the Christian faith say? In this passage from Colossians we can see a vision of unity, not in some scientific theorem or equation, nor in a pantheistic leveling where all is God, but in a person who brings it all together—Jesus Christ. By looking at some key phrases in this passage we can gain a more complete understanding of what our *universe* is truly about.

3

In the Image of God

The first thing we are told in this passage is that Christ is "the image of the invisible God" (v. 15). This immediately brings to mind the creation account where we are told that God made people "in His own image" (Gen. 1:17). Humankind was created to perfectly reflect God. Tragically, once people sinned that "image of God" became considerably blurred. It could also be argued that all of creation was made in God's image. Genesis tells us that all of creation was "good" (1:4,10,12,18,21,25), and Jesus declares that the word "good" should be used to describe God alone (Mark 10:18). The goodness of creation reflected the goodness of God. Psalm 19:1 says that even now, "The heavens declare the glory of God; the skies proclaim the work of his hands" (NIV). But with human sin, nothing could be said to be the exact image of God—until Christ came. When Christ came, He alone was the perfect reflection, the image of the invisible God. Hebrews 1:3 tells us that Christ "is the radiance of His [God's] glory, the exact expression of His nature." So Christ came as what God intended all of creation, and particularly humankind, to be—the exact representation of Himself. But that is not the end of the story. Verse 15 goes on to say that Christ is also "the firstborn over all creation." Christ leads the way for all of creation to return to what it was created to be—a reflection of the goodness of God.

today's session (cont'd)

Christ, the Nucleus

We also need to examine verse 17 more closely: "by Him all things hold together." As the nucleus is to the atom, so Christ is to all of creation. This isn't saying that Christ is a physical force like cosmic gravity, but rather He makes creation a unified whole. He is the one who makes the created order a *universe*. Without the hub of a wheel, the wheel will collapse. Without its nucleus, the electrons of an atom would fly off in all directions. Without Christ, the created order would indeed be "full of sound and fury, signifying nothing." In other words, Christ keeps the universe moving in the direction of God's purpose for it.

The Great Reconciler

Perhaps the most central verse of this passage is verse 20. It tells us that God seeks through Christ "to reconcile everything to Himself by making peace through the blood of His cross –whether things on earth or things in heaven." Again we note that the word "everything" is used instead of "all people." The point we need to understand is that when humankind sinned, all of creation was affected. It became less than what it was created to be. This is what Paul referred to in Romans 8:20-21, "For the creation was subjected to futility–not willingly, but because of Him who subjected it–in the hope that the creation itself will also be set free from the bondage of corruption into the glorious freedom of God's children." Creation has been in the "bondage of corruption" brought about by human sin. This explains our conflicting experiences with creation. We look at creation and see the beauty that God intended–the sunsets and rainbows, the majesty of mountains, and roaring ocean waves. But we also see much pain and destruction that God did not originally intend–violent deaths from storms, earthquakes, and the like; extinction of animals due to human abuse and neglect; pollution of all parts of our planet; and in general a life system in disharmony.

How did human sin affect the rest of creation?

In the midst of this great disharmony, Christ came as the great Reconciler, bringing peace and forgiveness by the blood of His cross. His blood provides the first step in taking things back to the way they were supposed to be. When Christ returns, He will complete this process, making heaven and earth new and eliminating the pain and death brought on by human sin (Rev. 21:1-5). He will be like a modern auto mechanic, tuning up a car according to preset computerized settings–except the "setting" Christ will use will be the perfection of Himself. Everything will need to be as good, harmonic, and loving as He is.

How did Christ's sacrificial death bring reconciliation to a world in disharmony?

A Personal Application

While Paul wrote about the universe, he did not want to be so big and expansive in scope as to forget the individual. In verse 22 he explained, "But now He has reconciled you by His physical body through His death, to present you holy, faultless, and blameless before Him." It all starts with the individual being reconciled to God through what Christ did on the cross—"by His physical body through His death." We cannot fully be part of making things right in the world until things are right within our own hearts. Some people in the church at Colossae thought this happened through the intervention of angelic beings, which Paul referred to disparagingly as "the elemental forces of the world" (2:8). We don't know much about this philosophy except that Paul said it was "based on human tradition." In any case, Paul issued a warning to stay away from false teaching and "remain grounded and steadfast in the faith" (v. 23)— the gospel that proclaimed salvation through the atoning death of Jesus Christ. Once we find this reconciliation then we can begin the work of helping our world toward reconciliation.

What do we need to do before helping our world toward reconciliation?

3

notes:

Remain in groups of 6–8 people, in a horseshoe configuration.

In this small-group session, students will be applying the lessons of the text to their own lives through the following questions.

The students were asked (in the student book) to choose an answer for each question and explain why.

Learning from the Story (5-7 minutes)

1. At what point in your life have you felt most alienated from God? How did this feeling of alienation affect your behavior?

2. How quick are you to feel blamed for certain bad things happening?

   ☐ Very quick—the evils of Nazi Germany were probably somehow my fault.
   ☐ Moderately quick—if in doubt, it was my fault.
   ☐ Moderately slow—I can be convinced by the evidence.
   ☐ Very slow—I thought I was wrong once, but I was mistaken!

3. What does it mean to you to be holy? How can you "remain grounded and steadfast in the faith" (v. 23)?

notes:

life change lessons (5-7 minutes)

Share with the class the following thoughts on how the lessons of this text might be applied today. The answers to the student book questions (provided in the margin) are underlined unless the question requires a personal answer.

If someone asked you, "Why can't we all just get along?" what would you answer?

A number of years ago after a controversial incident involving the use of violence by police against a black man, Rodney King, the victim in this incident, made his oft-quoted statement, "Why can't we all just get along?" This is a very complicated question, and we have seen in this session how the disharmony of sin has affected the entire universe. While God intended harmony and unity, sin has thrown everything into disarray. People do not get along with God. They do not get along with each other. And they are out of sync with their environment. Only Christ, the One who perfectly reflects God Himself, can bring us back together. That is the hope we are called to both proclaim and live out in our actions.

In applying today's lesson, then, we need to start with the basics and move ahead to the more advanced. Specifically, we need to:

1. MAKE SURE WE ARE PERSONALLY RIGHT WITH GOD. If you have not accepted Christ as your Savior, that is where you need to begin. When we are driven by disruption and disharmony within, we cannot help resolve the disruption and disharmony in the world. When we accept God's gracious forgiveness of our own spiritual weakness, then we can extend that grace to others.

What three things can a Christian do to find reconciliation with another person?

2. ACT THIS WEEK TO FIND PERSONAL RECONCILIATION WITH ONE OTHER PERSON. This can be a family member, a person at work, or anyone with whom you have been in conflict. Begin by hearing this person's story. Without using blame, share your feelings about the conflict that has arisen between you. Extend the forgiveness that God has given you to this person.

3. BECOME INVOLVED IN A MINISTRY OF RECONCILIATION. This can be anything from an environmental action group (reconciling people to the environment God has created), to a group working for peace in a troubled area of the world, to an evangelistic mission reconciling people to God. Choose one, not on the basis of what others say you ought to do, but on the basis of the passion and call that God gives you.

notes:

CARING TIME
Remain in groups of 6–8 people, in a horseshoe configuration.

Hand out the Prayer/ Praise Report to the entire group. Ask each subgroup to pray for the empty chair. Pray specifically for God to guide you to someone to bring next week to fill that chair.

After a sufficient time of prayer in subgroups, close in a corporate prayer. Say, "Next week we will talk about: 'Socially Unacceptable, Divinely Revered.'"

Remind participants of the daily Scripture readings and reflective questions found on page 44.

Caring Time (15-20 minutes)

Remember that this is the time for expressing your concern for each other as group members and for supporting one another in prayer. Begin by having each group member answer this question:

"With whom do you need to find reconciliation in the coming week? How can the group pray for you?"

Pray for these needs, as well as the concerns listed on the Prayer/ Praise Report. Remember to pray for God's guidance in inviting someone to the group next week to fill the empty chair.

notes:

BIBLE STUDY NOTES

Reference Notes

Use these notes to gain further understanding of the text as you study on your own.

COLOSSIANS 1:15

image of the invisible God. "Image" does not mean a second-hand representation (such as a photograph is an image of a person), but a complete representation: All that God is, Jesus is (John 1:18, 14:9; 2 Cor. 4:4-6; Heb. 1:3). To know God fully, you need not look anywhere else but to Christ.

firstborn. This term had nothing to do with Jesus being created, but meant that Jesus was like the first pioneer into the kingdom that will one day include all who come to God through Jesus.

COLOSSIANS 1:16

thrones or dominions or rulers or authorities. Christ is Lord over all authorities.

COLOSSIANS 1:17

He is before all things. Christ's preeminence means He is Lord over all.
by Him all things hold together. Both Greek and Jewish philosophers were concerned with the "first principles" that gave order and meaning to life. Paul asserts that this is found in Christ (John 1:9).

COLOSSIANS 1:18

the head of the body. This emphasizes the organic, living relationship between Christ and His people.
firstborn. As Jesus is Lord over the original creation, so also he is Lord over the new creation (v. 15).

COLOSSIANS 1:19

fullness. All that can be experienced of God is found in Christ.

COLOSSIANS 1:20

reconcile everything to Himself. Jesus seeks the eventual goal of not only reconciling humanity to Himself, but to creation, which has been thrown out of kilter by sin (Rom. 8:19-25).
the blood of His cross. The irony of the gospel is that this cosmic work of redemption was completed through the gory, earthly act of crucifixion.

COLOSSIANS 1:21

alienated. Jews viewed Gentile idolatry and immorality as the chief evidence that humanity was in revolt against God. Paul utilized that idea to contrast the Colossians' "before" and "after" status in Christ.
hostile in mind. "Mind" (like the Old Testament word for "heart") represents the core of the personality.

COLOSSIANS 1:22

His physical body. The stress is on Jesus' actual body that died, as opposed to the church as the expression of Christ's glorified body (1:18).
holy, faultless, and blameless before Him. While the false teachers taught that the Colossians needed something more in order to be truly spiritual, Paul used the language both of sacrifice and the law court to emphasize that believers are completely acceptable to God through Christ (Rom. 8:1-11).

COLOSSIANS 1:23

remain grounded and steadfast in the faith. The work of Christ must be received with faith demonstrated by an ongoing loyalty and obedience to Christ.
proclaimed in all creation under heaven. In face of what the false teachers had said, Paul reassured his readers that they had already received the full gospel as proclaimed everywhere else.

notes:

Session 4

Socially Unacceptable, Divinely Revered

Prepare for the Session

	READINGS	REFLECTIVE QUESTIONS
Monday	Colossians 1:24-29	How are you living your life so that others can see Christ in you?
Tuesday	Colossians 2:1-5	Who especially needs your encouragement today? What can you do to give that encouragement?
Wednesday	Luke 10:16	Why does having Christ in you sometimes result in rejection by others? How will you handle such rejection when it occurs?
Thursday	Mark 9:38-41	How have others supported and encouraged you as you have sought to live the Christian life?
Friday	John 14:19-21	How does knowing and remembering that Christ is in you help you to show greater obedience to Him?
Saturday	John 15:18-21	In what ways do you feel persecuted because you are a Christian? How does it help to know that Christ experienced the same things Himself?
Sunday	1 Peter 4:12-13	Have you come to the point where you can say you are glad to suffer for Christ's sake? Why or why not?

OUR GOALS FOR THIS SESSION ARE:

In groups of 6–8, gather people in a horseshoe configuration.

Make sure everyone has a name tag.

Take time to share information on class parties that are coming up as well as any relevant church events.

INTRODUCE THE ICEBREAKER ACTIVITY: The students have been given instructions in their books.

After the Icebreaker say something like, "Whether we like mysteries or not, the universe is full of them. Some people in the church at Colossae held some 'mysterious' perspectives, but Paul pointed them to the greatest mystery of all—Christ in us. In this session we will look at why this is a mystery and what solving the mystery means."

Hand out the Prayer/Praise Report. A sample copy is on pages 166-167. Have people write down prayer requests and praises. Then have the prayer coordinator collect the report and make copies for use during the Caring Time.

BIBLE STUDY
- to discover how Paul responded to the Greek mystery religions that were popular in Colossae
- to consider the role of suffering in furthering the gospel of Christ
- to learn what it means to have Christ in us and how that helps us to better follow Him

LIFE CHANGE
- to identify an area of our lives where acting on our faith is difficult
- to share our faith with one person with whom we have never shared it
- set aside time to call one person who needs encouragement

Icebreaker (10-15 minutes)

It's a Mystery to Me! Go around the group on question 1 and let everyone share. Then go around again on questions 2 and 3, as time allows.

1. How does reading or watching mysteries make you feel?
   - ☐ Stimulated—I always like to see if I can solve it before the detective.
   - ☐ Excited—I get wrapped up in the story.
   - ☐ Okay—but I prefer romances.
   - ☐ Depends on if anything gets blown up.
   - ☐ Bored—it's always the same formula stuff.
   - ☐ I just go to the last page first.
   - ☐ other: ______________________

2. To what real-life mystery would you most like to know the answer?
   - ☐ What really happened when JFK was killed?
   - ☐ Is the government actually hiding evidence of UFOs?
   - ☐ What happens to all those socks I lose so I wind up with half a pair?
   - ☐ Why does it always rain when I plan the picnic?
   - ☐ What is behind the disappearances in the Bermuda Triangle?
   - ☐ Did OJ really do it?
   - ☐ What do women want—really?
   - ☐ Why are men so clueless?
   - ☐ other: ______________________

4

Icebreaker (cont'd)

3. If your life were a mystery book, how would you title it?

notes:

LEARNING FROM THE BIBLE

COLOSSIANS 1:24–2:5

Have a member of the class, selected ahead of time, read Colossians 1:24–2:5.

Bible Study (30-45 minutes)

The Scripture for this week:

24Now I rejoice in my sufferings for you, and I am completing in my flesh what is lacking in Christ's afflictions for His body, that is, the church. 25I have become its minister, according to God's administration that was given to me for you, to make God's message fully known, 26the mystery hidden for ages and generations but now revealed to His saints. 27God wanted to make known to those among the Gentiles the glorious wealth of this mystery, which is Christ in you, the hope of glory. 28We proclaim Him, warning and teaching everyone with all wisdom, so that we may present everyone mature in Christ. 29I labor for this, striving with His strength that works powerfully in me.

1For I want you to know how great a struggle I have for you, for those in Laodicea, and for all who have not seen me in person. 2I want their hearts to be encouraged and joined together in love, so that they may have all the riches of assured understanding, and have the knowledge of God's mystery—Christ. 3In Him all the treasures of wisdom and knowledge are hidden.

4I am saying this so that no one will deceive you with persuasive arguments. 5For I may be absent in body, but I am with you in spirit, rejoicing to see your good order and the strength of your faith in Christ.

Summarize these introductory remarks. Be sure to include the underlined information, which gives the answers to the student book questions (provided in the margin).

What did all of the Greek mystery religions essentially teach?

To whom did Paul say the "mystery" of Christ in us was available?

What did old-line Judaism and the Greek mystery religions have in common in their teachings?

...about today's session (5 minutes)

THE MYSTERY OF CHRIST IN US

Like many people of modern times, those in ancient times seemed to love a mystery. In fact, many citizens of Rome and Greece practiced secretive religions known as "mystery religions." The essence of their teachings was that the great truths of life, including the nature of God and how to approach God, were mysteries revealed only to a few. These religions developed, in part, as a reaction to the more common Greek and Roman religions, which taught that a very undemanding collage of gods were available to everybody. The mystery religions were appealing because they were secretive and supposedly gave eternal access to an elitist group. Such a religious philosophy had apparently gained a strong foothold in Colossae, even in the church. To fight this perspective, Paul used some of the language of the mystery religions while putting a much different, Christian slant on it. Indeed a mystery–a previously unknown truth–had been recently revealed–"the mystery hidden for ages and generations but now revealed to His saints" (v. 26). But in spite of the implications some might see in those last two words, this was not a mystery reserved for an elitist group. If it had been, Paul would not have been broadcasting it in such a generally available letter. He would have reserved it to be taught in secret meetings or coded literature. This mystery was for the "saints," that is for all who chose to have faith in Christ, a choice available to all.

What was this mystery? It was the exact opposite of the exclusivism that the mystery religions and old-line Judaism taught. In Judaism God was available only to the Jews and not the Gentiles. In the mystery religions God was available only to those chosen to have the mystery revealed to them. But the Christian "mystery" is that the God of the universe could be within us–ALL of us–through Jesus Christ.

In today's session we will consider what it means that Christ can be in us and what "the glorious wealth of this mystery" (v. 27) can mean for us.

notes:

4

Remain in groups of 6–8 people, in a horseshoe configuration.

In this small-group session, students will be responding to the following questions that will help them share their stories in terms of the teaching of this passage in Colossians 1:24–2:5.

Have the students explore these questions together.

Identifying with the Story (5-7 minutes)

1. What have you labored for with the same energy that Paul had as he labored for his churches?

2. When do you remember getting a sense of fulfillment from serving someone else? What made this act of service fulfilling? In what ways were your feelings similar to Paul's?

3. Whose heart do you feel the need to encourage? Why is that person in extra need of encouragement?

notes:

Share with your class the following information which you may modify according to your own perspectives and teaching needs. The answers to the student book questions (provided in the margin) are underlined.

today's session (15-20 minutes)

At some point in life a follower of any religion or philosophy comes to the question, "Where do I fit in?" Even when we have a sense of the "big picture" of the universe, as we considered in last week's session, it means little if we don't feel we have a role in it all. In today's reading from Colossians, we see Paul looking specifically at his role, but also more generally at the role of the Christian in what Christ continues to do. We will look first at the role Paul saw for himself, and then we will consider our role.

Paul's Commission

Paul saw himself as called to fill what three roles?

Paul saw himself as called to fill three roles—suffering servant, proclaimer of the gospel, and encourager of believers. The role of suffering servant was first defined by Isaiah when he prophesied Christ's coming in Isaiah 53:4-5.

4

"Yet He Himself bore our sicknesses,
and He carried our pains;
but we in turn regarded Him stricken,
struck down by God and afflicted.

But He was pierced because of our transgressions,
crushed because of our iniquities;
punishment for our peace was on Him,
and we are healed by His wounds."

The early Christian community connected this prophecy strongly with Christ. Paul's claim to have inherited this role seems at first to be audacious. He wrote, "and I am completing in my flesh what is lacking in Christ's afflictions" (v. 24). How could Paul claim to fill what Christ lacked? How could he even claim that something Christ did was lacking? Paul did not claim that Christ's atoning act was insufficient to bring salvation. He did not say that Christ's crucifixion did not do something it was designed to do. Rather Paul emphasized that the redemption of creation would require followers of Christ to follow his example of suffering. This is taught many places in the New Testament: "Therefore, since Christ suffered in the flesh, arm yourselves also with the same resolve." "Instead, as you share in the sufferings of the Messiah rejoice, so that you may also rejoice with great joy at the revelation of His glory" (1 Pet. 4:1,13). "The Spirit Himself testifies together with our spirit that we are God's children, and if children, also heirs—heirs of God and co-heirs with Christ—*seeing that we suffer with Him so that we may also be glorified with Him*" (Rom. 8:16-17). Our suffering is important because by it we testify to the suffering love of Christ. Non-Christians who would

today's session (cont'd)

In what way did Paul's suffering "complete" the suffering of Christ?

otherwise not know of that suffering love, can know it when they see it in us. That is how Paul's suffering "completed" the suffering of Christ—by replicating it and making it known. He saw such suffering as part of being a servant of the gospel and of Christ's church.

Paul also saw himself as having the role of proclaiming the gospel—"We proclaim Him, warning and teaching everyone with all wisdom, so that we may present everyone mature in Christ" (v. 28). Right from the first, this was an important role given to all who would be disciples of Christ. Before His ascension Christ told His followers, "Go, therefore, and make disciples of all nations, baptizing them in the name of the Father and of the Son and of the Holy Spirit, teaching them to observe everything I have commanded you" (Matt. 28:19-20). Paul filled this commission perhaps better than anyone else, starting churches throughout Europe and Asia Minor.

What two things did Paul do regularly to encourage believers?

What two sources of pressure on early Christians made it especially important that they receive encouragement?

Finally, Paul saw his role as being an encourager of believers: "I want their hearts to be encouraged and joined together in love" (2:2). In our first session together we talked about how Paul nearly always began his letters with words of encouragement. But that was only part of it. He often personally went back to churches he had started with the sole purpose of encouraging them in their faith (Acts 14:21-22; 15:41; 18:23). We all need encouragement for any challenge we face, but these disciples were going through some very difficult times. They were under heavy pressure from friends and family members who held to traditional Jewish perspectives that rejected Jesus as the Messiah. In some parts of the Roman Empire they even came under physical persecution from Roman authorities. The persecution under Nero, during which Peter and Paul both were martyred, is the best-known example. Followers of Christ needed encouragement to know that they would receive a reward in the kingdom of God, which would make all hard times seem like nothing.

Our Role as Believers

In what ways might Christians of today have to suffer because of their faith?

We, too, are called to fulfill the same roles Paul felt called to fulfill. We are called to suffer for Christ. In our day and society we probably won't face physical death for our belief, though our generation has seen more Christian martyrs than any preceding one. However, Christians in our society who try to take their faith seriously do often face social castigation. Sometimes they lose their jobs for standing up for what Christ taught. Sometimes they even find themselves going to jail for such beliefs. It's all part of testifying to the suffering love of Christ through our own suffering. We are also called to proclaim Christ to those around us. Not all of us are to do this by preaching. For some of us it is simply a matter of talking to those closest to us about what Christ has done for us. Then finally we are called to encourage each other in the faith. All of us "hit bottom" sometimes. When that happens, we need someone who knows what we're going through to help us believe that we can make it through. This is why Alcoholics Anonymous and similar groups have been so successful. The church could aptly be renamed "Sinners Anonymous." We are all sinners who are strengthened by each other's support. Showing this kind of encouragement is a real need in our society today. That is why our television shows and movies often focus on the role of an encourager who helps a person reach higher than they previously reached: John Boy Walton is encouraged by his grandfather, among others; Luke Skywalker is encouraged by Obi-Wan Kenobi; William Forrester encourages a young black man to write in *Finding Forrester*; a soccer coach encourages a young woman of Indian heritage to play soccer in *Bend it Like Beckham*. These stories touch us because we all seek this kind of encouragement.

Paul used one more phrase that has great importance to our role. He writes, "God wanted to make known to those among the Gentiles the glorious wealth of this mystery, which is Christ in you, the hope of glory" (1:27). We are called to have Christ within us. That summarizes all that we are to be and do. On our own strength we fail repeatedly, but we don't have to rely on our own strength. In the *Star Wars* series, Luke Skywalker and others are repeatedly advised to "rely on the Force." Similarly, we are to rely on that presence of Christ within us to be strong in the faith. Such a strengthening power is not always rational or logical—it is a mystery. But that does not make it any less real. We have access to it through praying for that presence of Christ within us. We need to remember the closing sentence of the Great Commission, "I am with you always, to the end of the age" (Matt. 28:20).

notes:

Remain in groups of 6–8 people, in a horseshoe configuration.

In this small-group session, students will be applying the lessons of the text to their own lives through the following questions.

The students were asked (in the student book) to choose an answer for each question and explain why.

Learning from the Story (5-7 minutes)

1. Have you ever suffered for your faith? In what way? What does this passage say to you about that experience?

2. What "persuasive arguments" have you heard that pull people away from their hope in Jesus Christ? Which of these, if any, have given you the most trouble?

3. What does it mean to you to have "Christ in you" at this point in your life? What do you need to do to keep yourself aware of His presence and strength within you?

notes:

life change lessons (5-7 minutes)

Share with the class the following thoughts on how the lessons of this text might be applied today. The answers to the student book questions (provided in the margin) are underlined unless the question requires a personal answer.

Who comes to mind when you think of people who have suffered for their faith? Does their example encourage you to do the same or make you think they are somehow stronger and better than you could ever be?

Where does the power for doing things like suffering for our faith come from?

Today we looked at three areas where Paul sought to serve Christ—suffering for the benefit of His church, proclaiming the gospel, and encouraging believers. This presents three natural areas where we can act on today's lesson. However, if we just look at these areas of action we can feel intimidated. We almost wish that action opportunities were *not* clearly defined so we could have a good excuse to stay as we are. Suffering is hard, and few of us feel that we are made of the same stuff as Joan of Arc or Stephen (Acts 7:54-60) or the Christians thrown to the lions in the Roman coliseum. Witnessing for Christ is even more intimidating for many of us. And while encouraging others may seem less intimidating, we are still unsure how to do it sometimes. What if we can't do these things? Are we then fake Christians whom Christ will reject in the end? Rather than letting these roles intimidate us, we should concentrate on where the power for taking such roles comes from: Christ in us. We start by asking for Christ to come within us. Then we can let Him lead and empower us to face the world. Pointing to Christ we can say, "It's Him, not us!"

In applying today's lesson we need to start with inviting Christ to empower us. Then we can move on to these actions:

1. IDENTIFY AN AREA OF YOUR LIFE WHERE ACTING ON YOUR FAITH IS DIFFICULT. This might be (for example) standing up for ethics in the office where you work, speaking against Sunday morning tournaments with the coaches or group of parents of your child's baseball team, or working for a controversial piece of legislation that your friends oppose but which you believe is what Christ would want. Pray for Christ's presence as you take this action.

2. SHARE YOUR FAITH WITH ONE PERSON WITH WHOM YOU HAVE NEVER SHARED IT. Don't use high pressure. Just let the person know why you believe what you believe, and leave the rest to the Spirit.

3. SET ASIDE TIME TO CALL ONE PERSON WHO NEEDS ENCOURAGEMENT. Don't give a bunch of unsolicited advice. Just call to find out how the person is doing and listen. Let that person know you are praying for him or her, and then follow through with that promise. Assure this person that Christ can see him or her through any crisis.

notes:

CARING TIME
Remain in groups of 6–8 people, in a horseshoe configuration.

Hand out the Prayer/ Praise Report to the entire group. Ask each subgroup to pray for the empty chair. Pray specifically for God to guide you to someone to bring next week to fill that chair.

After a sufficient time of prayer in subgroups, close in a corporate prayer. Say, "Next week we will talk about: 'Nail It.' "

Remind participants of the daily Scripture readings and reflective questions found on page 56.

Caring Time (15-20 minutes)

Close by taking time to pray for one another and for your own special concerns. Begin by having each group member answer this question:

"In what area of your life do you need some encouragement this week?"

Pray for these needs, as well as the concerns on the Prayer/Praise Report. Include prayer that God would guide you to someone to invite for next week to fill the empty chair.

notes:

BIBLE STUDY NOTES

Reference Notes

Use these notes to gain further understanding of the text as you study on your own.

COLOSSIANS 1:24

completing in my flesh what is lacking in Christ's afflictions. Given Paul's stress on the once-for-all sufficiency of Christ's death as a sacrifice for sin (1:22), he could not mean that his sufferings somehow added to the value of Christ's death. Some believe he was alluding to Jewish apocalyptic tradition that anticipated a definite series of catastrophic events that must be experienced before the Messiah establishes the new world order. Since these events were related to the Messiah's appearance, they were known as the "woes of the Messiah."

COLOSSIANS 1:25

to make God's message fully known. This is another reminder that the gospel they have heard is indeed the complete gospel. There is nothing lacking that the false teachers can "fulfill."

COLOSSIANS 1:26

the mystery ... now revealed. These words may be allusions to Greek mystery religions that were popular at the time. Paul may have been using their language to show that the gospel is a better "mystery" than what they had been teaching. Such language could also have been borrowed from Jewish apocalyptic literature, which spoke of God's hidden mysteries whose meanings were revealed to only a few. God reveals the "mystery" of the gospel to all—including Gentiles—who believe. It is not a secret form of spiritual power, but the hope for eternity guaranteed by the presence of Christ within the believer.

COLOSSIANS 1:28

mature in Christ. The gospel message, which begins, continues, and ends with obeying Christ, is for all types of people who come to spiritual maturity through their day-to-day allegiance to Christ.

COLOSSIANS 2:1

Laodicea. A city located a short distance from Colossae (4:16).

COLOSSIANS 2:2

encouraged and joined together in love. The false teachers said there was a secret knowledge gained only by those few who practiced a variety of rites, experiences, or disciplines. Such a spirituality would naturally tend to discourage people and lead to factions. In contrast to such spiritual elitism, the gospel views spiritual growth as a growth in love for Christ and one another. This would lead to hope and shared fellowship.

notes:

Session

5

Nail It!

Prepare for the Session

	READINGS	REFLECTIVE QUESTIONS
Monday	Colossians 2:6-7	In what way has your faith been strengthened since starting this course?
Tuesday	Colossians 2:8-12	How susceptible are you to false and dangerous philosophies? How can you be less susceptible?
Wednesday	Colossians 2:13-15	Which sins or trespasses make you especially thankful that God has forgiven you? How can you show your thanks?
Thursday	Matthew 21:1-11	How was the triumphal entry of Christ into Jerusalem different from what the world calls triumph? How are you proclaiming Christ as King?
Friday	1 Corinthians 15:54-57	Have you let Christ have the victory over your own fear of death? Why or why not?
Saturday	1 John 5:4	What challenges in the world has your faith helped you overcome? What aspects of the world do you need more faith to master? How can Christ help you claim victory?
Sunday	Revelation 19:11-16	What will it mean when Christ truly reigns throughout the earth? What are you called to do to help?

OUR GOALS FOR THIS SESSION ARE:

In groups of 6–8, gather people in a horseshoe configuration.

Make sure everyone has a name tag.

Take time to share information on class parties that are coming up as well as any relevant church events.

INTRODUCE THE ICEBREAKER ACTIVITY: The students have been given instructions in their books.

After the Icebreaker say something like, "While we may have many important victories in our lives, as well as some significant losses, no victory is more important than being victorious in our spiritual lives. This is where the cross of Christ helps us triumph. We will consider how the cross helps us triumph in our session today."

Hand out the Prayer/Praise Report. A sample copy is on pages 166-167. Have people write down prayer requests and praises. Then have the prayer coordinator collect the report and make copies for use during the Caring Time.

BIBLE STUDY
- to fully understand the nature of the triumph we have through the cross of Christ
- to see the danger of false teaching and how it can rob us of our victory
- to discuss Christ's victory over spiritual powers and authorities

LIFE CHANGE
- to strengthen our commitment to regular personal Bible study
- to learn about and evaluate a competing philosophy
- to hold a personal forgiveness ceremony

Icebreaker (10-15 minutes)

Great Victories. Go around the group on question 1 and let everyone share. Then go around again on questions 2 and 3, as time allows.

1. What would you consider to be the greatest victory of your childhood or adolescence?

☐ learning to ride my bike
☐ beating out a rival for a certain guy or girl
☐ my sports team winning an important tournament
☐ getting cast for the role I wanted in a play or musical
☐ receiving an award for my music or art
☐ graduating from high school
☐ finally winning an argument with my parents
☐ receiving an important scholarship
☐ other: ____________________

2. If you could be assured of one victory in the coming year, what would you want it to be?

☐ to win "the battle of the bulge" and lose that extra weight
☐ to finally get the job I've been wanting
☐ to win a big contract I've been after
☐ to overcome an addiction
☐ to win the heart of a rebellious child
☐ to get a political leader I support elected
☐ to win an argument with my spouse
☐ to gain control of my finances
☐ other: ____________________

Icebreaker (cont'd)

3. Seeing your life in terms of a game you really want to win, where do you feel you are right now in the contest?
   - ☐ I'm way behind, with little or no chance of catching up.
   - ☐ I think there's a big "L" on my forehead.
   - ☐ I'm behind, but with hope of at least evening the score.
   - ☐ I'm winning about as much as I'm losing.
   - ☐ I'm ahead, but having to fight to stay that way.
   - ☐ I'm way ahead, and cruising to the finish line.

notes:

LEARNING FROM THE BIBLE

COLOSSIANS 2:6-15

Have a member of the class, selected ahead of time, read Colossians 2:6-15.

Bible Study (30-45 minutes)

The Scripture for this week:

6Therefore as you have received Christ Jesus the Lord, walk in Him, 7rooted and built up in Him and established in the faith, just as you were taught, and overflowing with thankfulness.

8Be careful that no one takes you captive through philosophy and empty deceit based on human tradition, based on the elemental forces of the world, and not based on Christ. 9For in Him the entire fullness of God's nature dwells bodily, 10and you have been filled by Him, who is the head over every ruler and authority. 11In Him you were also circumcised with a circumcision not done with hands, by putting off the body of flesh, in the circumcision of the Messiah. 12Having been buried with Him in baptism, you were also raised with Him through faith in the working of God, who raised Him from the dead. 13And when you were dead in trespasses and in the uncircumcision of your flesh, He made you alive with Him and forgave us all our trespasses. 14He erased the certificate of debt, with its obligations, that was against us and opposed to us, and has taken it out of the way by nailing it to the cross. 15He disarmed the rulers and authorities and disgraced them publicly; He triumphed over them by Him.

...about today's session (5 minutes)

Summarize these introductory remarks. Be sure to include the underlined information, which gives the answers to the student book questions (provided in the margin).

IN THIS SIGN CONQUER

An old tradition relates that once when the Roman Emperor Constantine was preparing to fight a battle, he saw a vision of a cross and heard a voice saying to him, "In this sign conquer." Following the advice, he hoisted the cross before his soldiers and went on to win the battle. From that time he became a Christian and eventually commanded all in his kingdom to be Christians as well. Some wonder whether this story is fully authentic, and others question whether forced Christianity was a boon or blessing. However, in a larger sense Christians would agree that "In this sign conquer" is a good theme for life. Through the cross we can conquer the challenges we face in life. This should not be taken in the sense of much modern American competition – beating out others or becoming one of the few winners, leaving many losers in our wake. Rather it means that we can win over the addictions, fears, compulsions, and temptations that seek to keep us from getting the most out of life and out of our relationships. Over such obstacles, ALL can become victors through Jesus Christ. If we follow them, some human forces and institutions will keep us from ever having such a victory, so we must win over these as well. Paul teaches us this in the text we will be looking at today. He promises "triumph" over the forces of the world that seek to bring us down (v. 15).

How is the victory we have in Jesus Christ different from competitive victories in sports?

In one sense the forces we fight today are different than those of Paul's time. Paul fought against a strange philosophy, a mystery religion, that is not prominent today. He fought against a dominant Roman government, which at his time was not friendly to Christians. He fought against the legalism of an entrenched Jewish leadership that had lost touch with loving people and bringing them to a loving God. But in another sense, we fight the same fight. We also fight against philosophies that pull people away from what Christ taught. We also fight sometimes against a government that seems to understand politics more than the visions of faith. And while we don't live in a country dominated by a legalistic Judaism, many in the Christian faith can be just as legalistic as Judaism ever was, and this can pull us from the truth of the gospel. In addition, human sin is human sin. It hasn't changed much through the ages. The good news is that the victory over sin which God promised through Paul is His promise to us as well.

What three forces did Paul fight against in his time?

How is what we fight against today similar to what Paul fought against?

In today's session we will consider what it means that we can find triumph through the cross of Christ.

Remain in groups of 6–8 people, in a horseshoe configuration.

In this small-group session, students will be responding to the following questions that will help them share their stories in terms of the teaching of this passage in Colossians 2:6-15.

Have the students explore these questions together.

Identifying with the Story (5-7 minutes)

1. When have you been taken "captive" by something or someone that, in the end, was deceitful?

2. When has being forgiven by someone given you a sense of freedom from captivity?

3. When have you felt the oppressiveness of debt? How is spiritual debt like financial debt? Which do you find more oppressive?

notes:

today's session (15-20 minutes)

Share with your class the following information which you may modify according to your own perspectives and teaching needs. The answers to the student book questions (provided in the margin) are underlined.

In any kind of contest of forces, to win you need to have a plan. Before a football or basketball game, sportscasters often visit with coaches to find out what their game plan is. Maybe in basketball the plan is to keep the ball out of the hands of a certain star player by double or triple-teaming him or her. In football, it may be running and controlling the ball so that the other team's passing attack does not have a chance to get on track. Similarly, a war requires a battle plan. The plan may be to use heavy bombing in an area to open the way for ground troops. Most often the way to victory involves sticking with the plan.

In our passage for today, Paul essentially told the Christians at Colossae to "stick with the game plan." "Therefore as you have received Christ Jesus the Lord, walk in Him, rooted and built up in Him and established in the faith, just as you were taught and overflowing with thankfulness" (vv. 6-7). He wanted to make sure that some false philosophy did not pull them away from God's plan and thus deprive them of their victory. Walking worthy of the Lord means sticking with what you are taught. If they would stick with the "game plan" in this way, they could be part of the triumph of Christ and the cross over three kinds of enemies: (1) false teaching, (2) sin and death, and (3) evil spiritual powers and authorities. Let's consider this three-fold triumph, one triumph at a time.

5

Over what three kinds of enemies can we triumph if we stick to the gospel we have been taught?

Triumphing over False Teaching

When you are in a battle, the enemy may take some of your soldiers captive. A well-known case in point from the recent conflict with Iraq is Jessica Lynch. Paul warns us in our passage for today, "Be careful that no one takes you captive through philosophy and empty deceit based on human tradition, based on the elemental forces of the world, and not based on Christ" (v. 8). Deceit is a common way that soldiers are taken captive. A trap is laid and soldiers are ambushed. Jessica Lynch was herself captured when her vehicle was ambushed after making a wrong turn. This is just the kind of thing that false teachers can do to Christians. They ambush you at your times of confusion. Paul was referring to teachers of one of the Greek mystery religions. The exact nature of this philosophy is not known, but it apparently included worship of angelic beings or "elemental forces of the world." These "angels" occupied a role that belonged to Christ. While we can only partially evaluate such a teaching of which so little is known, we can think of deceptive teaching of our present day. In the teaching of some so-called Christian groups, the Bible is used to teach the human tradition of racial superiority. To be taken captive by such a teaching is to surrender the picture of a kingdom where "There is no Jew or Greek, slave or free, male or female; for you are all one in Christ Jesus" (Gal. 3:28). In the teaching

What two modern false teachings are mentioned? Can you think of others?

today's session (cont'd)

of some, Christ was nothing more than a human teacher, like many other human teachers. To be taken by such an idea is to surrender the vision of "God with us," the Word made flesh (John 1:1-18). While we must not define legitimate Christian teaching so narrowly that we exclude any intellectual or spiritual searching or divergence of opinion, care must be taken to maintain the essence of historic Christian thought. Christian teaching must remain rooted in Christ (v. 7).

Triumphing over Sin and Death

What connection does Scripture make between sin and death?

Scripture clearly links sin and death. A prime example is Romans 5:12: "Therefore, just as sin entered the world through one man, and death through sin, in this way death spread to all men, because all sinned." Similarly Romans 6:23 reminds us, "For the wages of sin is death." The cross of Christ brings us triumph over both sin and death. On that cross Christ paid the penalty for our sin, and by so doing bought our forgiveness. Thus Paul tells us in verse 13, "And when you were dead in trespasses and in the uncircumcision of your flesh, He made you alive with Him and forgave us all our trespasses."

This triumph caused Paul to write in 1 Corinthians15:56-57, "Now the sting of death is sin, and the power of sin is the law. But thanks be to God, who gives us the victory through our Lord Jesus Christ!" What victory can be more important than a victory over sin and death? No fear enslaves a person more than the fear of death. From the moment we are old enough to truly understand that death in a physical sense is permanent, we worry either about a loved one dying or about our own death. But Christ's victory means that death does not have the last word. Our love relationships can be eternal in Jesus Christ. And a victory over sin is important not just because it brings us this victory over death. Many people are miserable in this life because they have allowed themselves to be defeated by their own weak sinful nature. They cannot resist their desires and have affairs that cost them their families. They are addicted to destructive behavior such as drug and alcohol abuse, so everything they have to build on in life falls in on them. A triumph over sin means that sin does not have to destroy our lives.

The essential thing to remember is that apart from Christ this victory over sin and death cannot happen. That is why false teaching which removes the focus of faith away from Christ is so dangerous. It can rob us of this important victory!

Triumphing over Powers and Authorities

What historical event in the spiritual or unseen realm indicates that the "rulers and authorities" Paul wrote about were not human rulers and authorities?

Our passage also tells us, "He disarmed the rulers and authorities and disgraced them publicly; He triumphed over them by Him" (v. 15). The final passage in the NIV may be a little clearer: "triumphing over them by the cross." Who are these "rulers and authorities" and what does such a triumph mean for us? The authorities Paul is referring to are not human authorities. At this point in time Paul could not have said that human authorities like the government of Rome had been "disarmed" or "disgraced." Paul was writing about what could be called spiritual "rulers and authorities" or spirits and demons who oppose God. They are the ones to which the mystery religion popular in Colossae sought to do homage. Paul was saying that when Christ died on the cross and rose again these powers were defeated and publicly disgraced. Like soldiers in a defeated army are paraded around in chains to their own humiliation, so the defeat of these spirits was made public and evident.

For us this means no power in the universe, physical or spiritual, can rob us of our victory in Jesus Christ. As Paul said in Romans 8:38-39, "For I am persuaded that neither death nor life, nor angels nor rulers, nor things present, nor things to come, nor powers, nor height, nor depth, nor any other created thing will have the power to separate us from the love of God that is in Christ Jesus our Lord!" Our victory is secure!

notes:

Remain in groups of 6–8 people, in a horseshoe configuration.

In this small-group session, students will be applying the lessons of the text to their own lives through the following questions.

The students were asked (in the student book) to choose an answer for each question and explain why.

Learning from the Story (5-7 minutes)

1. What causes people to turn away from the faith they are taught? How can Christians help each other become more firmly "rooted" and "established in the faith" (v. 7) so this is less likely to happen?

2. What does it mean to be "dead in trespasses" (v. 13)? How does Christ help make us alive again?

3. What evidence, if any, have you seen of evil spiritual "rulers and authorities"? What does it mean to you that such powers have been "disarmed" and "disgraced" (v. 15)?

notes:

Share with the class the following thoughts on how the lessons of this text might be applied today. The answers to the student book questions (provided in the margin) are underlined unless the question requires a personal answer.

life change lessons (5-7 minutes)

No victory can be won if you only *know* the strategy—you still have to *act* on it. We must do that with what we have learned in this passage. Acting in this case means some things we must *continue* to do, some things we must *avoid* doing, and some things we must *start* doing. We must continue holding to the faith we were taught when we first heard the gospel. This means periodically reviewing the basics of the Christian faith through Bible study and devotion. We must avoid getting taken in by false philosophies and religions. This means we must learn what they really teach and compare them with Scripture. And we must start taking seriously the power of evil in the world. That means not underestimating the "powers and authorities," which seek to move the world in another direction than what God plans. However, we must still affirm that no power or authority exists in heaven or in earth, in the physical world or in the spiritual world that God cannot defeat. That is indeed the kind of good news we can stake our lives on!

What victories has God won in your life? What victories does He still need to win?

In applying today's lesson, we specifically need to:

What debts did you owe before Christ paid them at the cross?

1. STRENGTHEN OUR COMMITMENT TO REGULAR PERSONAL BIBLE STUDY. We cannot stay "rooted" in what we were taught, without regular review of what that teaching is. If you are not spending regular time in personal Bible study, start. If you are already spending some time, try increasing the time by 5-10 minutes a day.

2. LEARN ABOUT AND EVALUATE A COMPETING PHILOSOPHY. Find out what the philosophy teaches. Does it conflict with what Christ teaches? In what way(s)? Make sure that you read what Christian writers have to say about the philosophy.

3. HOLD A PERSONAL FORGIVENESS CEREMONY. Write down on slips of paper various sins that have at one time or another burdened you with guilt. These may be things you did earlier in your life or things you did recently. Then reread verses 13-14, "And when you were dead in trespasses and in the uncircumcision of your flesh, He made you alive with Him and forgave us all our trespasses. He erased the certificate of debt, with its obligations, that was against us and opposed to us, and has taken it out of the way by nailing it to the cross." Then either burn these papers in a fireplace or tack them to a wooden cross. Say a prayer of thanks for the forgiveness you have received.

notes:

CARING TIME
Remain in groups of 6–8 people, in a horseshoe configuration.

Hand out the Prayer/ Praise Report to the entire group. Ask each subgroup to pray for the empty chair. Pray specifically for God to guide you to someone to bring next week to fill that chair.

After a sufficient time of prayer in subgroups, close in a corporate prayer. Say, "Next week we will talk about: 'Transformational Flow Chart.' "

Remind participants of the daily Scripture readings and reflective questions found on page 68.

Caring Time (15-20 minutes)

Remember that this time is for developing and expressing your caring for each other. Since we are called by our passage to be "overflowing with thankfulness" (v. 7), let's be in that spirit! Begin by having each group member answer this question:

"What are some victories God has given you for which you are especially thankful?"

Thank God for these victories, and then move on to praying for the concerns on the Prayer/Praise Report. Pray specifically for God to guide you to someone to bring next week to fill the empty chair.

notes:

BIBLE STUDY NOTES

Reference Notes

Use these notes to gain further understanding of the text as you study on your own.

COLOSSIANS 2:6

received Christ Jesus the Lord. To receive Jesus as "Lord" is to acknowledge Him as the supreme authority in one's life.

COLOSSIANS 2:8

philosophy and empty deceit. The false teachings were not based on the teachings of Christ, but upon faulty ideas influenced by the "basic principles" of the world, angelic beings that manipulated human affairs in opposition to God (1:16; 1 Cor. 2:6,8; Gal. 3:19; 4:3,9; Eph. 6:12).

COLOSSIANS 2:9

in Him the entire fullness of God's nature dwells bodily. While the false teachers related to fallen angelic beings, believers relate to God incarnate (1:19).

COLOSSIANS 2:10

you have been filled by Him. Believing in Christ, one needs to look nowhere else for any greater spiritual power, knowledge, or experience.

COLOSSIANS 2:11

circumcised. The false teachers' ascetic route to spiritual fulfillment included circumcision. This circumcision was probably not based on the Old Testament circumcision as a sign of obedience to the Law of Moses (Gal. 5:2-4), but on the Greek mystery religions that practiced circumcision as a symbol of being emancipated from the fleshly limits of the body in order to enter the realm of spiritual reality.

COLOSSIANS 2:13

when you were dead. Jesus' physical death is compared with the lack of spiritual life in the Colossians prior to their conversion (Eph. 2:1-10). ***uncircumcision.*** Paul countered that a physical act will not cure the problem of a *heart* that is not set apart for God. This is the same argument used in the Old Testament to call Jews to circumcise their hearts for God (Deut. 10:16; Jer. 4:4).

COLOSSIANS 2:14

the certificate of debt. This refers to a written agreement to pay back a debt or to obey a law. When fulfilled, the document was blotted out and canceled.

COLOSSIANS 2:15

triumphed over. Paul used the image of a conquering hero forcing the vanquished army to march after him in a victory parade.

notes:

Session

6

Transformational Flow Chart

Prepare for the Session

	READINGS	REFLECTIVE QUESTIONS
Monday	Colossians 2:16-19	On what matters are you letting others judge you? What would Christ say about this?
Tuesday	Colossians 2:20-23	In what ways are you letting yourself be tied up by regulations? How would Christ free you?
Wednesday	John 15:1-4	How is your connection to Christ resulting in your life "bearing fruit"?
Thursday	John 15:5-6	At what point(s) in your life have you found yourself withering away in isolation?
Friday	1 Corinthians 12:12-13	How does remaining connected to Christ, the Head, solidify your fellowship with others in the body, the church?
Saturday	1 Corinthians 12:27-30	How are you currently serving Christ with your gifts?
Sunday	Hebrews 10:24-25	What role does attendance at worship and other church events play in keeping you connected to Christ?

OUR GOALS FOR THIS SESSION ARE:

BIBLE STUDY	• to understand that Christ is the Head of the church and of each individual member • to consider the role of ascetic practices in Christian living • to evaluate the role negative rules play in how we are to act and live as Christians
LIFE CHANGE	• to evaluate who in our lives is pulling our guilt strings • to make this week's decisions with greater deliberation • to begin each day with a spiritual "Pledge of Allegiance"

In groups of 6–8, gather people in a horseshoe configuration.

Make sure everyone has a name tag.

Take time to share information on class parties that are coming up as well as any relevant church events.

INTRODUCE THE ICEBREAKER ACTIVITY: The students have been given instructions in their books.

After the Icebreaker say something like, "Most people today prefer to live their lives by positive principles to follow rather than by "don'ts" to avoid. That was true with Paul as well. Today's passage talks about a philosophy that tried to run people's lives by "don'ts." Paul sought to point people to a more positive way in Christ. Let's look at what he had to say."

Hand out the Prayer/ Praise Report. A sample copy is on pages 166-167. Have people write down prayer requests and praises. Then have the prayer coordinator collect the report and make copies for use during the Caring Time.

Icebreaker (10-15 minutes)

The Big "Don'ts" of Life. Go around the group on question 1 and let everyone share. Then go around again on questions 2 and 3, as time allows.

1. With which of the following "don'ts" did you have the hardest time when you were a child or adolescent?

- ☐ "Don't drink milk or juice right out of the carton!"
- ☐ "Don't talk with your mouth full!"
- ☐ "Don't talk back to your mother/father!"
- ☐ "Don't eat in the living room!"
- ☐ "Don't play that music so loud!"
- ☐ "Don't have friends over while we're gone!"
- ☐ "Don't talk to strangers!"
- ☐ "Don't pet stray dogs!"

2. Which of the following "do's and don'ts" best exemplifies the philosophy of the home where you were raised?

- ☐ "Don't do anything I wouldn't do."
- ☐ "Do unto others as you would have them do unto you."
- ☐ "Do unto others BEFORE they do unto you."
- ☐ "Do whatever you want, but don't get caught."
- ☐ "Don't get mad—get even."
- ☐ "If in doubt—don't."
- ☐ "Don't ask—don't tell."
- ☐ "Do your best."

3. If you had to choose one "don't" that you wish people today would observe more closely, what would it be?

6

LEARNING FROM THE BIBLE

COLOSSIANS 2:16-23

Have a member of the class, selected ahead of time, read Colossians 2:16-23.

Bible Study (30-45 minutes)

The Scripture for this week:

[16]Therefore don't let anyone judge you in regard to food and drink or in the matter of a festival or a new moon or a sabbath day. [17]These are a shadow of what was to come; the substance is the Messiah. [18]Let no one disqualify you, insisting on ascetic practices and the worship of angels, claiming access to a visionary realm and inflated without cause by his fleshly mind. [19]He doesn't hold on to the Head, from whom the whole body, nourished and held together by its ligaments and tendons, develops with growth from God.

[20]If you died with Christ to the elemental forces of this world, why do you live as if you still belonged to the world? Why do you submit to regulations: [21]"Don't handle, don't taste, don't touch"? [22]All these regulations refer to what is destroyed by being used up; they are human commands and doctrines. [23]Although these have a reputation of wisdom by promoting ascetic practices, humility, and severe treatment of the body, they are not of any value against fleshly indulgence.

notes:

...about today's session (5 minutes)

Summarize these introductory remarks. Be sure to include the underlined information, which gives the answers to the student book questions (provided in the margin).

WHO'S IN CHARGE HERE?

To what does failing to keep in touch with Christ as Head lead?

In the old comedy series *Third Rock from the Sun*, a group of aliens spied on earthlings and then reported their findings to a leader called "the Big Giant Head." The completion of their mission depended on regular contact with this "Big Giant Head." This is a comical equivalent of what Paul calls us to do in our Scripture. In all that we do we, as the body of Christ, are to keep in touch with Christ, the Head. Failing to keep in touch leads to forgetting who is in charge and therefore allows control by those who would use control to our detriment. Paul writes that the one who seeks to lead us away from Christ and toward other lifestyles, "doesn't hold on to the Head, from whom the whole body, nourished and held together by its ligaments and tendons, develops with growth from God" (v. 19).

What happens to the physical body when the neurological pathways to the brain are compromised? What are the implications when this dynamic occurs relative to a Christian or a church body?

In a physical sense, keeping in touch with the head helps the body act in ways that are coordinated and purposeful. Someone with neurological problems or nerve damage may act in an uncoordinated manner. Damage to the spinal cord can result in a person becoming a quadriplegic. The mind still sends the same signals, but they don't get through. Does Christ sometimes feel like a quadriplegic? He keeps sending messages to the church, but the church does not act! Or more frequently, some of the messages get through and some do not, leading to a church that acts in a spasmodic, uncoordinated way.

How can we keep the church of Christ acting as a body? It starts with making sure the church remains connected to the Head. Human leaders, while important, cannot replace that Head. Human philosophy, while at times helpful, cannot replace what Christ tells us. Christ must be the one in charge. A body with more than one head generally cannot survive. An organization with more than one head will degenerate into chaos and most often fall apart. The church of Christ cannot afford to let that happen.

If we split the role of "head" of our lives between Christ and anyone else, what can happen?

What is true of the church is also true of our lives. Our lives should have but one head–Jesus Christ. If we try to split that role between Christ and ourselves or between Christ and friends or even Christ and our human critics–we will become schizophrenic and divided in direction.

In today's session we will look at what it means that Christ is the Head of the church and of us, and at what can happen when we do not stay connected to the Head.

Remain in groups of 6–8 people, in a horseshoe configuration.

In this small-group session, students will be responding to the following questions. These questions will help them share their stories in terms of the teaching of this passage in Colossians 2:16-23.

Have the students explore these questions together.

Identifying with the Story (5-7 minutes)

1. In what area of behavior do you feel others are most likely to judge you?

   - ☐ what I eat or drink
   - ☐ my appearance—whether or not I'm "attractive," overweight, too thin, etc.
   - ☐ my fashion sense—styles like earrings, tattoos, hair coloring, etc.
   - ☐ my friends
   - ☐ the movies or television shows I watch
   - ☐ my political involvement
   - ☐ other: ______________________

2. When you feel others are judging you, how are you most likely to react?

   - ☐ I judge them in return.
   - ☐ I shrug it off.
   - ☐ I act even more eccentric.
   - ☐ I fly into a rage.
   - ☐ I try to be like they want me to be.
   - ☐ I take it to God in prayer.
   - ☐ I find out what my friends think.
   - ☐ other: ______________________

3. If Christ could say one thing to you about the way you are relating to the judgments and regulations others try to place upon you, what do you think He would say?

notes:

today's session (15-20 minutes)

Share with your class the following information which you may modify according to your own perspectives and teaching needs. The answers to the student book questions (provided in the margin) are underlined.

Can a person "take charge of his or her life" and have Christ as Head? What happens when we try to take charge of our lives without including Christ?

When we lose touch with Christ as the Head of our lives or the life of the church, someone comes in quickly to fill the void. It's like weeds that fill in bare spots left in your yard or garden. Perhaps the person filling in the space of leadership in your life is yourself. Is that bad? Don't people say, "Take charge of your life!"? The problem is that when we take control of our lives without direction from God, we quickly become directed by our sin. That sin is destructive to us as well as to others. What we need to do is take charge of our lives while letting Christ lead us to do what is best for all.

Other people allow their friends and colleagues to direct their lives. They allow themselves to be judged by the values and principles of others. In whatever they do they try to avoid the disapproval of others. This just leads to a kind of slavery to the other person's conscience. Whatever input Christ has is filtered through the distortions of that other person's perceptions. We cannot make Christ Head of our lives if we have already given that position to others.

What two problems result when we don't make Christ the undisputed Head of our lives?

To walk in a manner worthy of our Lord, we must make Christ the undisputed Head of our lives. If we don't look to Christ for leadership, two problems will result–unhealthy guilt and getting misled by false answers. Let's look at what Paul has to say about both of these.

Unhealthy Guilt

Why is normal guilt vital to healthy functioning as an adult?

The first problem that results from replacing Christ as Head is unhealthy guilt. Some psychologists, such as Freud, used to teach that all guilt was unhealthy. But in more recent times, psychologists have found that people with no sense of guilt are actually psychopaths who can kill without batting an eyelash. Normal guilt has a purpose. It is like physical pain. Just like physical pain warns you that you are doing something destructive to your body, so guilt is spiritual pain that warns you of damage to your spirit and relationships to others. However, some people turn normal guilt into unhealthy guilt. They try to make others feel guilty about what is not their fault. They also try to make others feel guilty about actions that are long behind them for which they have already asked forgiveness. They try to make others even feel guilty about normal acts that one should not feel guilty about at all. Apparently that was happening at Colossae. Paul wrote to the church there, "Therefore don't let anyone judge you in regard to food and drink or in the matter of a festival or a new moon or a sabbath day" (v. 16). This last phrase refers to Jewish annual, monthly, and weekly holy days. In Colossae these rituals were probably not being pushed by people of traditional Jewish faith, but rather by a syncretistic mystery religion that held them as essential.

today's session (cont'd)

In verse 17 Paul taught that such disciplines are just a "shadow of what was to come; the substance is the Messiah." That means eating restrictions and worship disciplines were earthly attempts to prepare people for the heavenly remedy for sin that came in Jesus. Hebrews 8:5 shows us that the priests and laws of the Old Testament "serve as a copy and shadow of the heavenly things." Hebrews 10:1 reinforces this: "Since the law has only a shadow of the good things to come, and not the actual form of those realities, it can never perfect the worshipers by the same sacrifices they continually offer year after year." This language of shadow, substance, and reality comes from Plato. His famous allusion was to a cave. What if a person lived his or her entire life in a cave and experienced only the shadows cast on a wall by the real people and real events passing by the door of the cave? Wouldn't such a person think the shadows were the reality? In Plato's mind that was exactly how things are. We experience only the shadows of a higher reality. Paul was using this to say that the Law (and implicitly other human systems meant for spiritual enlightenment) is just the shadow of the higher reality that came from heaven in Jesus Christ. When people reject the grace that comes through Christ for the legalism of human systems, they are rejecting spiritual reality (substance) in favor of grabbing at its shadows.

Upon what philosopher is Paul's language about shadow and substance based? For Paul, what is the "shadow" and what is the "substance"?

The picture then is that these adherents of a mystery religion were seeking to pull people's guilt strings over a system that was nothing but shadows in the first place. Rather than letting such misguided people tie us up in guilt over their regulations, we need to accept the grace of Jesus Christ. The grace of Jesus Christ takes us beyond all of the "don'ts" of life to something more. Yes, we should avoid some activities. But just avoiding the bad stuff is not what life is about. God wants us to experience His forgiveness when we go wrong. He wants to give us life in abundance (John 10:10).

False Answers

A second problem that results from replacing Christ as Head is getting misled by false answers. What these mystery religions taught were "human commands and doctrines" (v. 22). They were people's ways of solving a problem and not God's ways. They were intended to elevate the spirit by denying the flesh, but Paul warned that they promised what they could not deliver: "they are not of any value against fleshly indulgence" (v. 23).

Ascetic practices like fasting or setting aside worldly luxuries are *not* bad or unhelpful. Jesus fasted in the wilderness. He also called on the rich young ruler to sell everything he had to come follow Him (Matt. 19:21). Paul himself advised the use of strict disciplines, "Do you not know that the runners in a stadium all race, but only one receives the prize? Run in such a way that you may win. Now everyone who competes exercises self-control in everything. However, they do it to receive a perishable crown, but we an imperishable one. Therefore I do not run like one who runs aimlessly, or box like one who beats the air. Instead, I discipline my body and bring it under strict control, so that after preaching to others, I myself will not be disqualified" (1 Cor. 9:24-26). The difference between Paul's teachings and what these human philosophies taught was that Paul said that the essential thing was Christ, while ascetic practices were a helpful addition. On the other hand, the mystery religions were apparently teaching that the ascetic practices were the essential thing, while in their syncretism they were treating Christ as a helpful add-on. Paul insisted that ascetic practices by themselves could not do the trick: "they are not of any value against fleshly indulgence." It is Christ that is of ultimate value, as Paul confessed in Philippians 4:13: "I am able to do all things through Him who strengthens me."

What was the difference between Paul's teachings about ascetic practices and what the mystery religions of Colossae seemed to be teaching?

notes:

6

Remain in groups of 6–8 people, in a horseshoe configuration.

In this small-group session, students will be applying the lessons of the text to their own lives through the following questions.

The students were asked (in the student book) to choose an answer for each question and explain why.

Learning from the Story (5-7 minutes)

1. What does it mean to "live as if you still belonged to the world" (v. 20)? To whom do we belong?

2. Why are people so prone to get tied up in the "don'ts" of life? To what degree are the "don'ts" helpful, and to what degree are they insufficient?

3. What practices and attitudes have you found most helpful in restraining yourself from "fleshly indulgence" (overeating, addictive behavior, etc.)? How has Christ helped you?

notes:

life change lessons (5-7 minutes)

Share with the class the following thoughts on how the lessons of this text might be applied today. The answers to the student book questions (provided in the margin) are underlined unless the question requires a personal answer.

What must we do to develop an action plan for an abstract goal like keeping Christ as Head of our life?

One thing about the ascetic approach to life change is that it is easy to make a plan of action. Avoid this list of foods or drinks. Limit caloric intake to so much. Get these items or behaviors out of your life. One may not actually be able to *follow* the plan, but making it is relatively easy. However, how do you make a plan of action when the goal is to keep Christ as Head in your life? It seems a little too abstract. Nevertheless, it is similar to other goals we might set for our lives that are equally abstract. For instance, we might say that we want to strengthen our marriage or become a better parent. Such goals require that we think of what they might mean in terms of concrete actions. If our goal is to strengthen our marriage, an action goal might be to reserve one night a week to go out together. If our goal is to be a better parent, the action goal might be to spend 15 minutes daily in meaningful conversation with each of our children. We must develop some similar action goals to keep Christ as head of our lives.

The action goals we set to keep Christ as head must keep in mind what we have learned in our lesson today. Specifically, we need to avoid letting others determine the "do's" and "don'ts" of our lives, based on their own values and agenda. Rather we need to let Christ direct us in all that we do.

In applying today's lesson here are some specific, concrete suggestions:

1. EVALUATE WHO IS PULLING OUR GUILT STRINGS. Name all the times in the last several weeks when someone said or did something that resulted in you feeling guilty. Who is on your list more than once? Are the things this person wants you to do in accord with your own view of Scripture? Are they acting out of love or a desire to control you? In your prayer time, turn each instance over to Christ for His direction.

2. MAKE THIS WEEK'S DECISIONS WITH GREATER DELIBERATION. Before you make a decision, ask yourself, "Who am I thinking about pleasing in the way I am deciding this? Is it a parent? A spouse? A friend? Or is it Christ? Is this what Jesus would have me do? Why do I think so?"

As we begin each day, what can we do to help keep Christ as our Head?

3. BEGIN EACH DAY WITH A SPIRITUAL "PLEDGE OF ALLEGIANCE." During your morning devotional time, or at least before you begin your agenda for the day, turn your day over to Christ. You might stand before a cross or simply visualize Christ in your mind. Then say something like, "Jesus, You are my Lord. I pledge to let everything I do this day declare to all You are Lord of my life."

CARING TIME
Remain in groups of 6–8 people, in a horseshoe configuration.

Hand out the Prayer/ Praise Report to the entire group. Ask each subgroup to pray for the empty chair. Pray specifically for God to guide you to someone to bring next week to fill that chair.

After a sufficient time of prayer in subgroups, close in a corporate prayer. Say, "Next week we will talk about: 'Phenomenal Focus.' "

Remind participants of the daily Scripture readings and reflective questions found on page 80.

Caring Time (15-20 minutes)

Close by praying for one another. Begin this time by having each group member answer this question:

"What issue are you facing in the coming week for which you will need Christ's direction as Head of your life?"

Pray for Christ's direction on these issues, and then move on to praying for the concerns on the Prayer/Praise Report. Continue to pray for God's guidance on whom to invite to fill the empty chair.

Notes:

BIBLE STUDY NOTES

Reference Notes

Use these notes to gain further understanding of the text as you study on your own.

COLOSSIANS 2:16

eat or drink. Ascetic practices were common in ancient religions. In this context, the reason for such practices appears to have been to attune oneself to the "elemental spirits" that controlled the world.

a festival or a new moon or a sabbath day. These events serve as a summary of the annual, monthly, and weekly Jewish holy days (1 Chron. 23:31). Pagans also observed cycles of worship determined by astrological practices. The false teachers probably used the Jewish traditions to support their astrological calendar.

COLOSSIANS 2:17

a shadow ... the substance. Hebrews 8:3-13 and 10:1-18 use this Platonic imagery to describe the work of Christ as compared to the Old Testament sacrificial system (see also 1 Cor. 5:7). While the false teachers claimed their ascetic practices were the pathway that led to the reality of spiritual experience, Paul asserted that they only lead to the shadowlands and not to a true spiritual life.

COLOSSIANS 2:18

ascetic practices. Paul was obviously not repudiating a true humility before God, but rather had in mind the ascetic practices, like enforced fasting, which mask pride with a facade of humility.

worship of angels. Since there is little evidence of a cult of angels at this time, the false teachers may have claimed their spiritual elevation allowed them to worship the Deity in the company of the angels.

access to a visionary realm. Inscriptions in pagan temples used this phrase to refer to a rite that authorized a person to be a teacher of the divine mysteries.

COLOSSIANS 2:19

the Head. Having abandoned Christ as their authority, the false teachers were not part of the body (the church).

COLOSSIANS 2:20

died with Christ. Elsewhere, Paul used the image of dying with Christ to show how the believer's bond to sin (Rom. 6:16-18,23) and to the Law (Rom. 7:1,4) is broken. Here, he used it to show that their bondage to the "elemental forces" had also been severed. Since the power of the forces has been severed, it is foolish to submit to their authority as a route to spiritual life (Gal. 4:1-11).

COLOSSIANS 2:23

promoting ascetic practices. The problem here is not ascetic practices as spiritual disciplines. Jesus himself fasted in the wilderness for 40 days. The problem seems to be that there were those in Colossae who taught that such practices were necessary for salvation. This emphasis then replaced their reliance on Christ.

notes:

Session

7 Phenomenal Focus

Prepare for the Session

	READINGS	REFLECTIVE QUESTIONS
Monday	Colossians 3:1	What attitude taught by your parents do you need to reaffirm?
Tuesday	Colossians 3:2-4	On what is your mind usually focused—on the heavenly or the earthly? How can you focus more on "what is above"?
Wednesday	Colossians 3:5	What worldly passions do you struggle with the most? What needs to happen for you to have a victory over these passions?
Thursday	Colossians 3:6-7	What moral issues that tempted you once has Christ helped you overcome? Have you thanked Him for these victories?
Friday	Matthew 6:19-21	What is your "investment strategy" for investing in things that are eternal?
Saturday	Matthew 16:21-23	How is your mind's focal point reflected in your attitude toward suffering and death?
Sunday	1 Corinthians 9:24-25	Are you "running the race" for a heavenly prize or an earthly one? What does this imply for how you discipline yourself?

OUR GOALS FOR THIS SESSION ARE:

BIBLE STUDY	• to understand the importance of focusing on spiritual values rather than worldly ones • to consider what it means to die to self and come alive to Christ, and how this can help us deal with temptations • to realize the value of setting spiritual goals to let Christ truly control our lives
LIFE CHANGE	• to compose a personal life mission statement • to define life goals for the next five years • to set two to three objectives for each life goal for the next five years

In groups of 6–8, gather people in a horseshoe configuration.

Make sure everyone has a name tag.

Take time to share information on class parties that are coming up as well as any relevant church events.

INTRODUCE THE ICEBREAKER ACTIVITY: The students have been given instructions in their books.

After the Icebreaker say something like, "While as adults we may not have to deal as much with the wrath of our parents, we do have to deal with the wrath of God. Although the New Testament portrays God as patient and loving, that does not mean He never gets angry. What God gets angry about and how He expresses that anger is part of what we will be looking at in our session today."

Hand out the Prayer/ Praise Report. A sample copy is on pages 166-167. Have people write down prayer requests and praises. Then have the prayer coordinator collect the report and make copies for use during the Caring Time.

Icebreaker (10-15 minutes)

Parental Wrath. Go around the group on question 1 and let everyone share. Then go around again on questions 2 and 3, as time allows.

1. When you were a child, which of the following would have been most likely to stir up your parents' wrath against you?

- ☐ talking back to them
- ☐ lying
- ☐ not getting my chores done
- ☐ making a mess
- ☐ making too much noise
- ☐ other: ____________
- ☐ playing, fighting, or rough-housing indoors
- ☐ inviting friends over without asking
- ☐ watching TV instead of doing homework

2. Which of the following images best describes how your parents expressed their anger? Put an "M" by the answer for your mother and an "F" by the answer for your father.

____ like a volcano—dormant for long periods, then exploding without warning
____ like a wounded grizzly bear—destroying all in its wake
____ like a mama lion—using a few well-placed growls and swats
____ like an angry bird—chirping and fluttering all over the place, but doing little damage
____ like an angry house cat—stay out of his way and you're okay, but get too close and you get your face sliced
____ like an injured bunny—quietly hiding away in some corner of the cage

7

Icebreaker (cont'd)

3. What more than anything else incites you to wrath as an adult?

notes:

LEARNING FROM THE BIBLE

COLOSSIANS 3:1-7

Have a member of the class, selected ahead of time, read Colossians 3:1-7.

Bible Study (30-45 minutes)

The Scripture for this week:

[1]So if you have been raised with the Messiah, seek what is above, where the Messiah is, seated at the right hand of God. [2]Set your minds on what is above, not on what is on the earth. [3]For you have died, and your life is hidden with the Messiah in God. [4]When the Messiah, who is your life, is revealed, then you also will be revealed with Him in glory.

[5]Therefore, put to death whatever in you is worldly: sexual immorality, impurity, lust, evil desire, and greed, which is idolatry. [6]Because of these, God's wrath comes on the disobedient, [7]and you once walked in these things when you were living in them.

notes:

...about today's session (5 minutes)

Summarize these introductory remarks. Be sure to include the underlined information, which gives the answers to the student book questions (provided in the margin).

GETTING DOWN TO SPECIFICS

In an old *Peanuts* cartoon, Linus tells Charlie Brown that he wants to be a doctor. Charlie Brown responds by telling Linus that he couldn't be a good doctor because he doesn't love humanity. Linus' classic response is: "I love humanity! ... It's PEOPLE I can't stand!" This reminds us that as long as we are talking generalities, we can agree to any set of principles. But what happens when it comes to specifics like loving an actual person? To this point in our letter, Paul has been mostly talking about generalities—walking in a manner worthy of the Lord, being agents of reconciliation, holding on to the faith we have been taught, holding on to Christ as Head. In our session for today, he starts with a generality ("seek what is above"), but then he continues with very specific instructions about what he wants the Colossians to do and not do. They are to avoid sexual immorality, impurity, lust, evil desire, and greed. It is in following specifics like this that "the rubber hits the road" in relation to whether we really can walk in a manner worthy of our Lord.

Why is it important to go beyond the generalities to the specifics of what Christ calls us to do and not do?

When we start talking about specifics like this, many Christians get nervous. "I'm not sure I can avoid all of those things! I'm too weak and human." It makes us especially nervous when Paul says, "Because of these, God's wrath comes on the disobedient" (v. 6). In this session we need to look at how we take on the challenge of these specific demands of the Christian life when we are weak human beings.

7

What societal influences are mentioned as making it harder to follow what Christ wants? What in our society makes it harder for you to live up to the specific behavioral demands of Jesus Christ?

Our challenge is even harder because we live in a society obsessed with the behaviors and attitudes we are supposed to be avoiding. Sexual immorality has seemingly infected every aspect of our society. Not only are our movies, television shows, and popular songs full of references to promiscuous sex, but sex is the basis for much of our business advertising. Not only are many of our business and political leaders involved in sex scandals, but so are many of our trusted religious leaders. In the midst of so much failure in this area we need a source of hope and help. If anything, we are doing even worse in the area of greed. Our economy is based on greed. Business thrives by getting people to want more and more things that they don't have. If you have a nice car, you can't be happy until you have a nicer SUV. If you have a computer, you can't be happy until you have the *latest* computer with the most RAM. If you have a cell phone, you can't be happy until you have one that can take and transmit pictures. Our society says, "Because of these things, the economy thrives." Scripture says, "Because of these, God's wrath comes on the disobedient." In this session we will address the challenge of this contrast.

How does society's attitude toward greed contrast to that of Christ?

Remain in groups of 6–8 people, in a horseshoe configuration.

In this small-group session, students will be responding to the following questions that will help them share their stories in terms of the teaching of this passage in Colossians 3:1-7.

Have the students explore these questions together.

Identifying with the Story (5-7 minutes)

1. Which of the following statements best expresses the attitude toward Christ with which you were raised?
   - ☐ He was at the center of our family's life.
   - ☐ We relied on Him to pull us through in hard times.
   - ☐ We sought to honor and obey Him.
   - ☐ We paid homage to Him at Easter and Christmas.
   - ☐ He was one we knew about, but mostly ignored.
   - ☐ We rejected Him.
   - ☐ His name was mostly mentioned in our swearing.

2. Were you to leave this earthly life today what, besides people, would you have the hardest time leaving behind?

3. When it comes to focusing your life on Christ instead of earthly things, in which of the following circumstances do you have the hardest time?
   - ☐ when I'm in a shopping mall
   - ☐ pretty much always
   - ☐ when I see what my neighbors or coworkers have
   - ☐ when I'm where there are a lot of attractive people of the opposite sex
   - ☐ when I'm watching commercials on TV
   - ☐ when I'm visiting someone else's really nice home
   - ☐ pretty much always
   - ☐ other: ____________

notes:

today's session (15-20 minutes)

Share with your class the following information which you may modify according to your own perspectives and teaching needs. The answers to the student book questions (provided in the margin) are underlined.

The behaviors and attitudes Paul told the Colossians to avoid are basically the same as what Judaism had been calling people to avoid for a long time. In contrast to Greek and Roman society, Judaism held to a high sexual ethic. Proverbs called again and again for young men to avoid "loose women" and to be true to the wife of their youth. The laws of the Pentateuch gave strict penalties for those caught in adultery or involved in deviant sexual acts. Greed also was condemned. The prophet Amos condemned Israel for "selling the righteous for silver and the needy for a pair of sandals" (Amos 2:6, NIV). Lending at interest was also forbidden (Lev. 25: 35-37), and laws were made for the periodic forgiveness of debt. Ecclesiastes wisely taught, "Whoever loves money never has money enough; whoever loves wealth is never satisfied with his income" (Eccl.. 5:10, NIV).

What does Paul teach here regarding wrong attitudes? How does that compare to what Jesus taught about such things?

If anything, Paul called for even more stringent behaviors and attitudes than the teachings of Judaism. He picked up on the teaching of Jesus who taught, "But I tell you, everyone who looks at a woman to lust for her has already committed adultery with her in his heart" (Matt. 5:28). We must avoid evil attitudes as well as evil acts. And so Paul demanded that we avoid "lust" and "evil desire." He added an important attitudinal element to greed—"idolatry." Indeed, greed becomes idolatry because people end up worshiping money and things instead of the one true God.

This creates a problem for us. If people were not able to follow such stringent demands under Judaism, how can we do any better under Christianity? What assistance is offered to help sinful human beings address these behavioral and attitudinal demands? If violation results in God's wrath, what hope do we have?

First of all, nothing said here contradicts the New Testament teaching of grace. While our actions and attitudes deserve condemnation, God's mercy and grace give us salvation. Our text also points to actions we can do and attitudes we should have to help us live up to these standards. Let's look at our text to discover these actions and attitudes.

Dying to Self

What does it mean to "die to self"?

Notice verse 3, "For you have died, and your life is hidden with the Messiah in God." This is an allusion to Jesus' teaching: "Anyone finding his life will lose it, and anyone losing his life because of Me will find it" (Matt. 10:39). When we die to self and come alive to Christ we really learn what life is. Dying to self means we no longer focus primarily on what benefits the self, but on what benefits Christ. Now

today's session (cont'd)

that does not make turning away from lust and greed suddenly easy. The self has a way of reasserting itself. However, the discipline of focusing on Christ can help a great deal because where we focus is likely to determine how we act. Some dieting plans use this issue of focus. If we focus on the foods we are giving up, our approach to dieting is going to fail because we eventually reach out to what we have focused on. Our focus should rather be on eating healthy. Then our thinking isn't on what we are giving up but on enjoying what we are eating. In a similar manner, if our lives focus is on what exalts Christ and not on what satisfies our selfish nature, we won't be thinking about all that the self is giving up. Thus Paul wrote in Romans 8:6, "For the mind-set of the flesh is death, but the mind-set of the Spirit is life and peace."

Letting Christ Come Alive in Us

The second, even more important, part of this strategy is letting Christ come alive in us. Paul proclaimed in verses 3-4, "your life is hidden with the Messiah in God. When the Messiah, who is your life, is revealed, then you also will be revealed with Him in glory. He referred not only to an identification with Christ, but much more to Christ's presence actually being within us. We give our lives over to Christ, and Christ becomes our lives.

How does the presence of Christ within us help with attitudes like lust and greed?

The presence of Christ within us gives us an inner spiritual strength that we wouldn't otherwise have. That is why, referring to this presence of Christ within, Paul wrote in Philippians 4:13, "I am able to do all things through Him who strengthens me." "All things" includes being able to resist the allure of greed and lust.

Setting Spiritual Goals

What does "setting our minds on what is above" imply for setting life goals?

Having a victory over the negative behavior and attitudes that Paul talked about is not just a matter of what to avoid, but also what to seek. Paul calls us to "seek" and "set our minds" on what is above. That means we need to set radically different goals than our society encourages us to set. Our society generally encourages more material goals. A common goal is to make a certain amount of money in our career. Generally a person coming out of college today going into a professional career wants to make at least $50,000 a year. A six-figure income is considered the bare minimum for success by many, and the most aggressive young people coming out of college want to make their first million by the time they are 30. Others set their goals according to what they want to have—a luxury car like a Lexus or BMW; a resort condominium in a place like Cabo San Lucas,

Maui, or Cancun; a yacht, etc. When our only goals are set according to earthly standards of performance, greed is the natural result.

We don't need to rid ourselves of all goals for economic performance. But where are our spiritual goals? Do they control the greed factor in our economic goals? What kind of person do we want to be by the time we are 30? What spiritual skills do we want to have? What do we want to accomplish for Christ and the kingdom of God? Setting such goals is part of setting our minds on what is above. Our spiritual goals should include how and what we want to learn (reading so much of the Bible, attending so many classes or spiritual growth groups, successfully maintaining daily family devotions, etc.); what we want to do (be involved weekly in a ministry to the homeless, regularly visit shut-ins or those in the hospital); and the relationship we want to have with God (feel confident of our salvation, no longer feel plagued by guilt, have peace and joy in our lives). Over time we usually learn to hit the targets for which we aim. As Christians we can aim for nothing less than a life that pleases God.

What three areas of our lives might spiritual goals include?

notes:

7

Remain in groups of 6–8 people, in a horseshoe configuration.

In this small-group session, students will be applying the lessons of the text to their own lives through the following questions.

The students were asked (in the student book) to choose an answer for each question and explain why.

Learning from the Story (5-7 minutes)

1. What does it mean to you that your life is "hidden with the Messiah in God" (v. 3)? How does this help with temptation?

2. What do you now see as the most important weapon you have in your arsenal to deal a "death blow" to the behaviors and attitudes Paul refers to here: sexual immorality, impurity, lust, evil desire, and greed?

3. If greed is "idolatry," what or who would Christ say you are truly worshiping right now? Are you making yourself susceptible to receiving God's wrath?

notes:

life change lessons (5-7 minutes)

Share with the class the following thoughts on how the lessons of this text might be applied today. The answers to the student book questions (provided in the margin) are underlined unless the question requires a personal answer.

What are the elements of long-term planning?

Most organizations today engage in some kind of "long-term planning." Such planning generally involves examining the corporate "mission statement," setting general goals from that mission statement, and then prioritizing yearly concrete objectives that will help them realize their goals within a certain time period, perhaps 5 to 10 years. The objectives are concrete and measurable so that the organization can determine if they have met them or not. Christians can follow this same pattern. A personal mission statement can help us say in concrete form what our lives are about. It can be something we post in our home, room, or office that can remind us what our lives are about. From this mission statement we can outline perhaps three life goals that we want to accomplish in the next 5 to 10 years. Then based on these life goals we can write specific objectives. By such specific planning we can live out Paul's teaching to "set your minds on what is above." Families may want to make working on these goals and objectives a family project. A weekend family retreat can be planned to work through the specifics. Individuals may also want to find a place to get away for a retreat.

In applying today's lesson and doing some long-term planning, here are some specific, concrete suggestions:

How should a Christian prepare for writing a life mission statement?

1. COMPOSE A PERSONAL LIFE MISSION STATEMENT. This should not just be done off the top of our head. It should be preceded by a time of prayer and scriptural study. It needs to deal with the basic issue of what God wants to do with your life. What Scripture passages do you find that seem to particularly call you? What gifts and skills do you have from God that He wants you to use for Him? Getting input from other Christians who know you well may be helpful in this regard. What do they see as your strengths? How have they seen God using you in the past? This statement, once composed, should be no longer than two or three sentences. You may want to post it somewhere so it can serve as a daily reminder to you what your life is about. Whatever you do, don't just compose it and then forget about it!

2. DEFINE LIFE GOALS FOR THE NEXT FIVE YEARS. Examples might be something like, "I will become confident in my knowledge of the Bible as a source for spiritual direction"; "I will take the lead in having my family discuss the spiritual issues that confront their lives"; "I will become involved in a ministry to the homeless." These goals must help you to accomplish your life mission.

7

life change lessons (cont'd)

3. SET TWO TO THREE OBJECTIVES FOR EACH LIFE GOAL FOR THE NEXT FIVE YEARS. For instance, if you set the life goal of becoming confident of your Bible knowledge, you may want to have the objective of reading through the Bible twice in those five years. You may also want to have an objective of spending two hours each week in group Bible study. If your goal is to help the family confront spiritual issues together, an objective might be to have at least one half-hour family Bible study each week. Write these objectives down and evaluate the progress you are making on a regular basis.

CARING TIME
Remain in groups of 6–8 people, in a horseshoe configuration.

Hand out the Prayer/ Praise Report to the entire group. Ask each subgroup to pray for the empty chair. Pray specifically for God to guide you to someone to bring next week to fill that chair.

After a sufficient time of prayer in subgroups, close in a corporate prayer. Say, "Next week we will talk about: 'Managing Mad.' "

Remind participants of the daily Scripture readings and reflective questions found on page 92.

Caring Time (15-20 minutes)

Take time now to care for one another through prayer. Today we want to care for each other by supporting the process of overcoming temptation. Begin by having each group member finish this sentence:

"The 'evil desire' I am having the most difficulty with right now is ..."

Pray for the strength and presence of Christ to give you the victory over these desires. Then move on to praying for the concerns on the Prayer/Praise Report.

Pray specifically for God to guide you to someone to invite for next week to fill the empty chair.

notes:

BIBLE STUDY NOTES

Reference Notes

Use these notes to gain further understanding
of the text as you study on your own.

COLOSSIANS 3:1

raised with the Messiah. As the Christian's death-with-Christ cut the bonds to the old authorities (2:20), so one's life-with-Christ creates new bonds with God and others. "Messiah" is the Hebrew equivalent of the Greek word "Christ."

seek what is above. This is not encouraging escapism from earthly affairs. The point is that Christians are to shape their lives by the values of the heavenly world in which Christ sits enthroned as King, rather than heeding rules based on the elemental spirits.

COLOSSIANS 3:3

hidden with the Messiah in God. Why might a person's life need to be "hidden"? The allusion is to protection. In Exodus 33:22, God tells Moses that he will hide him in the cleft of a rock while His glory passes by. The sin-infected Moses needed to be protected from the glory of the sinless God, because sinful man cannot see God and live. Jesus is the "rock" in which we "hide" to protect us from the judgment of a righteous God. This is particularly relevant because the passage later refers to the wrath of God coming to judge evil behavior and attitudes (v. 6).

COLOSSIANS 3:5

put to death. Believers are to daily turn away from attitudes and actions that reflect the old way of life. worldly. Worldly attitudes and behaviors disregard God and follow selfish desires.

greed, which is idolatry. Jewish teachers frequently identified greed with idolatry. Paul says in 1 Timothy 6:10, "For the love of money is a root of all kinds of evil, and by craving it, some have wandered away from the faith and pierced themselves with many pains."

COLOSSIANS 3:7

you once walked in these things. Paul was writing to Greeks who had lived in a society that was relatively unrestrained in terms of sexual morals. Paul similarly warns the Christians of Corinth not to go back to their former licentious ways in 1 Corinthians 6:9-11. He knew that backsliding is a constant danger for a reformed life, as many in AA and other modern addiction groups have also learned.

notes:

Session

8

Managing Mad

Prepare for the Session

	READINGS	REFLECTIVE QUESTIONS
Monday	Colossians 3:8	Does your everyday language reflect the Lord you serve?
Tuesday	Colossians 3:9-10	When was the last time you lied to someone you cared about? How could you have dealt with the situation more honestly?
Wednesday	Colossians 3:11	What cultural differences are you allowing to separate you from others who are part of Christ's body?
Thursday	2 Corinthians 5:17	In what ways have you become someone new since you gave your life to Christ?
Friday	Ephesians 4:22-24	What have you done to change your "former way of life" and the harmful behaviors that were part of your pre-Christ life?
Saturday	Ephesians 4:25	Are you part of a Christian community where you can truly be honest with each other? What can you do to make truth and honesty more a part of your new way of being?
Sunday	Ephesians 4:26-27	Are you able to express your anger without sinning and deliberately hurting others?

OUR GOALS FOR THIS SESSION ARE:

In groups of 6–8, gather people in a horseshoe configuration.

Make sure everyone has a name tag.

Take time to share information on class parties that are coming up as well as any relevant church events.

INTRODUCE THE ICEBREAKER ACTIVITY: The students have been given instructions in their books.

After the Icebreaker say something like, "Most people tell what we call 'little white lies.' While we sometimes feel these are justified, Scripture calls us to a higher standard. We are to put lying away, along with sinful expressions of anger. Can we really do that? That is what we will be looking at in this session."

Hand out the Prayer/Praise Report. A sample copy is on pages 166-167. Have people write down prayer requests and praises. Then have the prayer coordinator collect the report and make copies for use during the Caring Time.

BIBLE STUDY	• to consider how a person who seeks to be a new person in Christ should handle anger • to understand the importance of truth and honesty in the Christian community • to affirm the need to break down walls between people of different cultures
LIFE CHANGE	• to keep an "anger diary" for a week and observe how we deal with anger • to confidentially reveal something personal to a trusted friend • to become better acquainted with a Christian of another race or culture

Icebreaker (10-15 minutes)

Liar, Liar, Pants on Fire! Go around the group on question 1 and let everyone share. Then go around again on questions 2 and 3, as time allows.

1. Which of the following lies do you remember your parents catching you in when you were a teen?
   - ☐ "Party while you were gone? What party?"
   - ☐ "Sure, I've finished my homework."
   - ☐ "Yes, there will be parental supervision."
   - ☐ "I'm just going to the library."
   - ☐ "That smell of cigarettes?—It must have been from the people around me."
   - ☐ "How should I know who broke it?"
   - ☐ "All of the other parents are letting their kids do it."
   - ☐ "I have no idea who brought those filthy magazines into the house!"

2. Which of the following lies do you find yourself telling most frequently today?
   - ☐ "The check is in the mail."
   - ☐ "Of course I trust you!"
   - ☐ "Sure I liked it. I'm just full."
   - ☐ "Angry? I'm not angry!"
   - ☐ "Sure! That dress looks great on you!"
   - ☐ "You should have seen the one that got away!"
   - ☐ "Why, I've never even looked at another man/woman!"

8

Icebreaker (cont'd)

3. What kind of liar would you say you are?
   - ▢ Terrible!—I always give it away in my eyes or voice.
   - ▢ Really bad—I feel guilty until I confess.
   - ▢ Okay—I can do it when I feel I have to.
   - ▢ Pretty good actually—I can get by with most lies I tell.
   - ▢ Pathological—I sometimes lie for no reason at all!
   - ▢ other: ____________________

notes:

LEARNING FROM THE BIBLE

COLOSSIANS 3:8-11

Have a member of the class, selected ahead of time, read Colossians 3:8-11.

Bible Study (30-45 minutes)

The Scripture for this week:

8But now you must also put away all the following: anger, wrath, malice, slander, and filthy language from your mouth. 9Do not lie to one another, since you have put off the old man with his practices 10and have put on the new man, who is being renewed in knowledge according to the image of his Creator. 11Here there is not Greek and Jew, circumcision and uncircumcision, barbarian, Scythian, slave and free; but Christ is all and in all.

notes:

Summarize these introductory remarks. Be sure to include the underlined information, which gives the answers to the student book questions (provided in the margin).

...about today's session (5 minutes)

MAKING PERSONAL CHANGE REAL

Most of us have resolved to change something in our lives but then have not quite gotten it done. We make a New Year's resolution to lose weight or to give up an addictive behavior but then give up before the end of January! We have all the best intentions, but somehow we keep going back to being the same old person. Is change really possible? Albert Einstein is reported to have claimed it is easier to change the nature of plutonium than the evil nature of humankind. Going much further back, Jeremiah said, "Can the Ethiopian change his skin or the leopard its spots? Neither can you do good who are accustomed to doing evil" (Jer. 13:23, NIV). Still Scripture calls us to be new people.

What overall goal does this passage give us for our spiritual growth?

Making such changes real can seem especially hard when we consider specific behavior like not letting our anger control us or becoming truthful people. We will be looking at those behavioral changes in our session today. In previous sessions we have already seen how we need Christ within us for such change to happen, and in this context we need to be reminded of that truth. Also, as we discussed last session, we need to have some specific goals for spiritual change. The teaching in our passage for today gives us an overall goal for our spiritual growth—to be renewed "according to the image of [our] Creator" (v. 10). That's a pretty high goal! But which is better, to set high goals that challenge us or easily attainable goals that make little impact on our lives? The story is told of a man who was driving through a rural area. He was amazed to see on every barn a bull's-eye with an arrow right in the center of it. He thought that the people around there must be amazing at archery. He stopped and asked a man about it. The man explained, "Oh, that's nothing. We just shoot an arrow at the barn. If it sticks, we draw a bull's-eye around it!" Some people set their goals in the same way. Whatever they hit they draw their target around. Those who set goals in this manner will never improve! God sets some demanding targets for us to hit—getting rid of our sinful expressions of anger, telling the truth to each other, and living as one with the people around us. Change can start by accepting demanding challenges such as these.

What is the problem with first seeing what we achieve and then claiming that was our goal all along?

What are three behavioral "targets" that God sets before us through this passage?

notes:

8

Remain in groups of 6–8 people, in a horseshoe configuration.

In this small-group session, students will be responding to the following questions that will help them share their stories in terms of the ethical demands of Colossians 3:8-11.

Have the students explore these questions together.

Identifying with the Story (5-7 minutes)

1. In which of the following ways are you most likely to express your anger?
   - ☐ I'm a yeller.
   - ☐ I hit and throw things—be sure to duck!
   - ☐ You don't want to hear the words I use.
   - ☐ I generally just talk it out.
   - ☐ I go running or take it out on the tennis court.
   - ☐ I get back at the one I'm angry at.
   - ☐ I try not to think about it.
   - ☐ I just seethe and quietly hold on to my anger for days.
   - ☐ other: ______________________

2. Finish this sentence: "The one thing I most wish I could change about the way I express my anger is ..."

3. To whom do you have the hardest time telling the truth?
   - ☐ my friends—I don't want to hurt their feelings.
   - ☐ my spouse or significant other—If I told him/her the truth, they would get mad.
   - ☐ customers—I need their business.
   - ☐ the government—They expect it.
   - ☐ strangers I do business with—It's not like I really care about them.
   - ☐ my parents—They just wouldn't understand.
   - ☐ other: ______________________

notes:

today's session (15-20 minutes)

Share with your class the following information which you may modify according to your own perspectives and teaching needs. The answers to the student book questions (provided in the margin) are underlined.

In today's competitive job market, people are becoming adept at writing resumes and adapting them to specific job descriptions. What is the "job description" for the follower of Christ? What kind of resume should one write to match that job description? Of course, in the writing of this resume "embellishing" the facts is just not going to work. The One to whom we apply already knows us better than we know ourselves, and we won't slip anything past Him! Also, on this resume "job history" does not matter so much. With Christ the past is part of the "old self" anyway. The new self and what that new self is doing right now is what matters. Let's look at three essential job qualifications for the new self and how a prospective candidate can develop them. These job qualifications include anger management, truthful relationships, and openness to all people.

What are three essential "job qualifications" for the new self in Jesus Christ?

Anger Management

One of the most important skills is learning how to manage anger. Paul tells us to "put away all the following: anger, wrath, malice, slander, and filthy language from your mouth" (v. 8). These are all different forms of mismanaged anger. While we are told to put away "anger," Paul does not mean we should never get angry about anything. We are dealing with an inadequacy of language here with one word ("anger") meaning many different things. Jesus Himself got angry. He drove the moneychangers out of the temple (Matt. 21:12-13) and frequently spoke angrily at the scribes and Pharisees. Paul showed anger in his letters (e.g., Gal. 1:6-10). In Ephesians 4:26 Paul warned, "Be angry and do not sin." In other words, it's okay to be angry, but just don't express that anger in a sinful way. In our anger we must not deliberately hurt another person. That is the implication of the word "malice." We must try not to use words that hurt or destroy others. Paul emphasized this when he called us to put away "slander" and "filthy language" from our mouth.

What are two examples of Jesus getting angry?

8

You can mismanage anger in two ways: expressing it in hurtful ways, as we have already mentioned, and holding it within while it turns into bitterness. The second part of Ephesians 4:26 tells us, "Don't let the sun go down on your anger." In other words, the new self who seeks to be "renewed in the image of his Creator" needs to resolve anger quickly so the relationship can be restored. The truthfulness verse 9 calls us to show is actually part of this. When we deal with anger in a truthful, straightforward way, we are most likely to resolve it quickly. In the movie *Anger Management* with Adam Sandler and Jack Nicholson, humor results when a man whose own anger is really out of control (Jack Nicholson) tries to teach an

What are two ways to mismanage anger?

today's session (cont'd)

apparently mild-mannered man (Adam Sandler) how to manage anger! Eventually we see that this supposedly mild-mannered man also mismanages anger because he doesn't know how to express it. Paul is telling us that the new person in Christ needs to learn to manage anger in a healthy and honest way.

We need to add that "honesty" in this sense does not mean making a vicious verbal attack on the person in the guise of being honest. We have already said that slandering and using hurtful or filthy language is inappropriate. What we need to aim for is honestly expressing our feelings, while also sharing the positive hope that the issues can be worked through and the relationship restored.

Truthful Relationships

A second "job qualification" for the new self is to be able to have truthful relationships. Paul taught, "Do not lie to one another, since you have put off the old man with his practices and have put on the new man" (vv. 9-10). This is a pretty stringent standard. He didn't say, "Do not lie to one another—unless you are trying to spare the other person's feelings." He didn't say, "Do not lie to one another—unless you are trying to be pleasant." He especially didn't say, "Do not lie to one another—unless you really need to save your ego." Paul simply said, "Do not lie to one another." This is important because a true relationship of love does not exist if it is based on facades. If you are not really being yourself and I am not really being myself, how can we say we love each other? We do not even know each other! As in all things, Jesus gives us the perfect example to follow. He was not afraid to tell even His closest disciples when they had disappointed Him. He showed His anger at Peter when Peter sought to deter His mission to die in Jerusalem (Matt. 16:23); He showed His disappointment with James and John when they asked for special honors (Mark 10:35-46); and He got angry with all of the disciples for the slowness of their understanding (Matt. 17:14-21). And yet His willingness to show His true self is what made it all the more meaningful when He declared His love and called the disciples His "friends" (John 15:12-15).

In what ways did Jesus set an example for us by being truthful with His disciples?

Openness to All

The final "job qualification" of the new self can best be described as openness to all people in Jesus Christ. Verse 11 says, "Here there is not Greek and Jew, circumcision and uncircumcision, barbarian, Scythian, slave and free; but Christ is all and in all." The new person in Jesus Christ can have no room for pairing Christian faith with ideas of racial superiority, ethnic cleansing, or acts of hate toward people of another race. To see Christ clearly is to see the One who unites all in a family of love. First John 3:14-15 reminds us, "We know that we have passed from death to life because we love our brothers. The one who does not love remains in death. Everyone who hates his brother is a murderer, and you know that no murderer has eternal life residing in him."

What are some of the divisions between people that Christ can help us heal?

We live in a world divided by racial and cultural barriers: black against white, Jew against Arab, Irish Catholic against Irish Protestant, English-speaking against Spanish-speaking. How can we testify to the world of God's love if we perpetuate the world's divisions? In the '80s the Berlin Wall was broken down. Perhaps the new millennium is a time for those who love Christ to break down these other walls. Paul teaches us, "For He is our peace, who made both groups [Jew and Gentile] one and tore down the dividing wall of hostility" (Eph.. 2:14). That is truly a task for new people in Christ.

notes:

8

Remain in groups of 6–8 people, in a horseshoe configuration.

In this small-group session, students will be applying the lessons of the text to their own lives through the following questions.

The students were asked (in the student book) to choose an answer for each question and explain why.

Learning from the Story (5-7 minutes)

1. Which of the following would you consider to be "filthy" language? Which is most offensive to you?
   - ☐ language with bathroom references
   - ☐ language with slang sexual references
   - ☐ language that takes God's name in vain
   - ☐ language that is hateful to another race or culture
   - ☐ language that puts others down

2. What reason is given for why we should not lie to one another (vv. 9-10)? Why should this be a deterrent to lying?

3. Had Paul been writing today, what groups might he have included in verse 11? What can Christians do to help bring such groups together?

notes:

life change lessons (5-7 minutes)

Share with the class the following thoughts on how the lessons of this text might be applied today. The answers to the student book questions (provided in the margin) are underlined unless the question requires a personal answer.

Wouldn't it be wonderful if becoming a new self was like ordering a new car? With a new car order you can stipulate color, engine size, and accessories (air conditioning, power locks, moon roof, cruise control, etc.). With an order for a "new self," instead of ordering "cruise control" you could order "anger control." Instead of tinted or clear windows you could designate a clearer window to your soul, so people could truly see who you are. Of course, things don't work that way in real life, but it can still be helpful to have a "shopping list" of things you want to see changed. Such a shopping list at least gives you the goals you want to reach. Our text for today adds some important traits to our "new-self" shopping list–the control of our anger, a new honesty, and a new openness to people of other races and cultures.

What are three important traits that our text adds to our "new-self shopping list"?

Ordering a new car must also be done with thoughts on how to accomplish the financial transaction. Will you have to finance it? If so, over how many months and at what interest rate? Getting a new self does not have to be financed, however, because Christ has already paid the price! He has brought forgiveness for the old self, laying the groundwork for the coming of the new self. This doesn't mean we don't have to do some planning, however. We need to think of how these changes will be accomplished.

What is God's "financing plan" for getting a new self?

Here are some suggestions of specific ways to apply this week's lesson:

1. KEEP AN "ANGER DIARY" FOR A WEEK, AND OBSERVE HOW YOU DEAL WITH ANGER. Write in it at the end of each day, and include all of the times you got angry about something. What made you angry, and how did you express (or not express) that anger? Are you still feeling angry at the end of the day? What did you learn about what gets you angry and how you deal with it? At the end of the week, write down at least two things you have learned about how you deal with anger and two suggestions to yourself how you might deal with it in a more Christian manner.

2. CONFIDENTIALLY REVEAL SOMETHING PERSONAL TO A TRUSTED FRIEND. This should be something you previously had not revealed because you were unsure how you might be received. Pray ahead of time about the person you need to trust with this information. Afterward, think the experience through. Was it harder or easier than you thought it would be? How do you feel now that you have done this?

life change lessons (cont'd)

3. BECOME BETTER ACQUAINTED WITH A CHRISTIAN OF ANOTHER RACE OR CULTURE. Meet over coffee, have lunch together, or converse over the Internet. What things do you find you have in common? What are the differences? What can you learn from the differences? What do these differences say to you about the body of Christ?

CARING TIME
Remain in groups of 6–8 people, in a horseshoe configuration.

Hand out the Prayer/ Praise Report to the entire group. Ask each subgroup to pray for the empty chair. Pray specifically for God to guide you to someone to bring next week to fill that chair.

After a sufficient time of prayer in subgroups, close in a corporate prayer. Say, "Next week we will talk about: 'Unmistakable Unanimity.' "

Remind participants of the daily Scripture readings and reflective questions found on page 104.

Caring Time (15-20 minutes)

Take this time to encourage and care for one another in prayer. Today we want to care for each other by sharing some of the things that are irritating us and which we need to get off our chest. Begin by finishing this sentence:

"Right now, I am feeling most angry about ..."

Pray for the strength and understanding to deal with these anger issues. Then move on to praying for the concerns on the Prayer/ Praise Report.

Pray specifically for God to guide you to someone to invite for next week to fill the empty chair.

notes:

BIBLE STUDY NOTES

Reference Notes

Use these notes to gain further understanding of the text as you study on your own.

COLOSSIANS 3:8

anger, wrath. The Greek word translated "anger" most often refers to a sudden flare of temper, while the Greek word for "wrath" most often refers to a lingering hostility.

filthy language. The implication here may actually be closer to "abusive language."

COLOSSIANS 3:9

put off the old man. Literally, "to strip off." This phrase is also used to describe the putting off of the sinful nature through Christ's death (2:11), and Christ's victory over spiritual powers (2:15).

COLOSSIANS 3:10

put on the new man. The lifestyle of Christians is patterned after the attitudes and actions of Christ who is at work within them (1 Cor. 15:45; Gal. 3:27).

according to the image of his Creator. In this letter we have already read that "the image of the invisible God" is Jesus Christ (1:15). So to be formed in the image of our Creator is also to be conformed to Jesus Christ.

COLOSSIANS 3:11

Scythian. The Greeks considered Scythians to be especially uncouth barbarians. Allegiance to Christ eradicates prideful divisions based on race, religion, culture, or social class (and gender—Gal. 3:28).

notes:

Session 9

Unmistakable Unanimity

Prepare for the Session

	READINGS	REFLECTIVE QUESTIONS
Monday	Colossians 3:12-13	Whom do you need to forgive today?
Tuesday	Colossians 3:14-15	When was the last time you felt "a perfect bond of unity" with the people around you? What was it that helped you to feel this way?
Wednesday	Colossians 3:16-17	What are you doing to celebrate all that Christ has done for you? Can those around you tell how thankful you are?
Thursday	Romans 2:23-24	What have you done recently that reflected poorly on your witness for Christ? Is there anything you might do to counteract this negative witness?
Friday	Matthew 18:21-35	How can your forgiveness toward others serve as a witness to what Christ has done for you?
Saturday	Matthew 10:40-42	What act of kindness can you do this week in the name of Jesus?
Sunday	John 20:21-23	Are you busy doing what Christ has sent you out to do?

OUR GOALS FOR THIS SESSION ARE:

In groups of 6–8, gather people in a horseshoe configuration.

Make sure everyone has a name tag.

Take time to share information on class parties that are coming up as well as any relevant church events.

BIBLE STUDY
- to understand more fully the role of loving others in our Christian walk
- to appreciate the need for Christian unity in witnessing to Christ
- to see why thanking God is essential to honoring the name of Christ

LIFE CHANGE
- to do one "servant task" around our home that we are not used to doing
- to forgive one person we have had conflict with in the church
- to make a list of all we have to be thankful for

Icebreaker (10-15 minutes)

INTRODUCE THE ICEBREAKER ACTIVITY: The students have been given instructions in their books.

After the Icebreaker say something like, "Many people find peace hard to find in today's world. In part it's because they are not even sure what they are looking for. In today's session we will talk about the peace that comes when we live and act in Jesus' name."

Hand out the Prayer/ Praise Report. A sample copy is on pages 166-167. Have people write down prayer requests and praises. Then have the prayer coordinator collect the report and make copies for use during the Caring Time.

Peace Signs. Go around the group on question 1 and let everyone share. Then go around again on questions 2 and 3, as time allows.

1. Where are you most likely to go when you are seeking a little peace in your life?
   - ☐ out in my car for a drive
   - ☐ my office with the phones on silent ring
   - ☐ a favorite retreat in the mountains or countryside
   - ☐ to a special little park
   - ☐ a favorite fishing hole
   - ☐ a chapel or sanctuary
   - ☐ The bathroom is my only refuge.
   - ☐ my garden
   - ☐ the golf course
   - ☐ I have no such place.
   - ☐ other: ____________

2. Which of the following descriptions of "peace" means the most to you?
   - ☐ no deadlines to have to meet
   - ☐ meaningful activity
   - ☐ a sense of accomplishment
   - ☐ a sense of belonging
   - ☐ confidence in the future
   - ☐ no painful memories to deal with
   - ☐ nobody harassing me to do stuff I don't want to do
   - ☐ a sense of oneness with the world and nature

Icebreaker (cont'd)

3. What would make the most relevant "peace sign" for your life?
   - ☐ a mountain—It speaks of the majesty of God.
   - ☐ a rainbow—Peace has often come after my storms.
   - ☐ the traditional peace sign—Peace in the world and peace within go hand in hand for me.
   - ☐ a dove—It calms me and reminds me of the Holy Spirit.
   - ☐ a beautiful sunrise—It speaks of the hope of tomorrow.
   - ☐ the cross—Peace comes from the release of my guilt.
   - ☐ other: ____________________

notes:

LEARNING FROM THE BIBLE

COLOSSIANS 3:12-17

Have a member of the class, selected ahead of time, read Colossians 3:12-17.

Bible Study (30-45 minutes)

The Scripture for this week:

12Therefore, God's chosen ones, holy and loved, put on heartfelt compassion, kindness, humility, gentleness, and patience, 13accepting one another and forgiving one another if anyone has a complaint against another. Just as the Lord has forgiven you, so also you must forgive. 14Above all, put on love—the perfect bond of unity. 15And let the peace of the Messiah, to which you were also called in one body, control your hearts. Be thankful. 16Let the message about the Messiah dwell richly among you, teaching and admonishing one another in all wisdom, and singing psalms, hymns, and spiritual songs, with gratitude in your hearts to God. 17And whatever you do, in word or in deed, do everything in the name of the Lord Jesus, giving thanks to God the Father through Him.

...about today's session (5 minutes)

Summarize these introductory remarks. Be sure to include the underlined information, which gives the answers to the student book questions (provided in the margin).

What are four situations where we might be called upon to honor the name of a group we represent?

How is the way of Christ's follower to be different from the way of the world?

Why do people who try to exalt their own names often wind up empty?

HONORING THE NAME

We all find ourselves in situations where we have to think about how our behavior reflects on the name of another person or on the organization with which we are affiliated. As children or teens we are reminded of how our behavior reflects on the family name. If we represent a company, all that we do affects how prospective customers see our company. If we are in the armed forces, all that we do and say affects how people see our country. That can even be true when we are traveling as private citizens in a foreign land. What is true in these situations is also true when we bear the name of Jesus Christ. Today's text tells us, "whatever you do, in word or in deed, do everything in the name of the Lord Jesus" (v. 17). We should do all that we do to glorify the name of Jesus Christ. Our study of Colossians is about walking worthy of the Lord. To live to glorify the name of Jesus is another way of saying the same thing.

The way of the world is to live to glorify one's own name. So many people want to be like the sports figure, singing star, or movie idol whose name is so recognizable that sometimes only one name is necessary: Elvis, Cher, Madonna, Ichiro, Shaq. Perhaps if everyone knows our name, we will feel important and valued. But as is so often learned, having a recognizable name does not assure that one will feel valued for one's self (as opposed to one's money or influence). Many celebrities, when they are honest with themselves, find such adulation rings a little hollow. They know in their heart that they are not worthy of the attention given them. John Lennon, before his death, took several years away from the limelight just to be with his family. He felt this was necessary to avoid what happened to Elvis Presley who had gotten so caught up with the public adulation that he had lost touch with who he was. The people most in touch with themselves realize that true praise belongs only to the One greater than all of us.

When we live to honor the name of Jesus, we are honoring the One to whom true praise belongs. In today's session we are going to look at what that means.

notes:

Remain in groups of 6–8 people, in a horseshoe configuration.

In this small-group session, students will be responding to the following questions that will help them share their stories in terms of the Christian qualities found in Colossians 3:12-17.

Have the students explore these questions together.

Identifying with the Story (5-7 minutes)

1. Which of the qualities in verses 12-13 do you have the hardest time "putting on"?
   - ☐ heartfelt compassion—feeling deeply the need of others
   - ☐ kindness—doing little acts to help, with no expectation of anything in return
   - ☐ humility—realizing it isn't all about me
   - ☐ gentleness—showing sensitivity so as not to wound others
   - ☐ patience—giving others time to change and grow
   - ☐ forgiving others—not holding on to old grudges

2. How would you describe the "bond of unity" that exists in your church fellowship?
   - ☐ Perfect—we are held together by the strength of God's love.
   - ☐ Strong, though not perfect—like "super-glue."
   - ☐ Uneven—some places are holding together better than others.
   - ☐ Pulling apart—like hardened old glue.
   - ☐ Not holding at all—like using flour paste on metal parts.

3. What "psalms, hymns, and spiritual songs" especially speak to you? What is there about these expressions that touches your heart or especially expresses what you feel toward God?

notes:

Share with your class the following information which you may modify according to your own perspectives and teaching needs. The answers to the student book questions (provided in the margin) are underlined.

today's session (15-20 minutes)

In our last session we looked at some behaviors for Christians to *avoid*: anger, filthy language, and lying. Today's Scripture passage leads us to some positive attitudes and behaviors to *cultivate*: love, unity, and thankfulness. These are all part of a life that testifies to the glory of Jesus' name. Today Jesus' name gets treated in many different ways by many different people. Many use it as a swear word or part of a phrase used in swearing. The reason why Christians get upset by this is because something precious is being used for a banal purpose. It's like taking the finest silk cloth and using it to wipe toilets. But it is also true that some Christians don't truly honor Jesus' name either. They call on Him with their lips, but not with their lives. Jesus said of these, "Why do you call Me 'Lord, Lord,' and don't do the things I say?" (Luke 6:46). Truly honoring Jesus' name is living according to what He taught. Let's look more closely at what this means.

What are two ways that Jesus' name is abused today?

Putting On Love

The Bible says, "Above all, put on love—the perfect bond of unity" (v. 14). Paul told the Ephesians to "Put on the full armor of God" (Eph.. 6:11). We put on love as our greatest weapon in a different kind of battle, a battle against hate and violence. "Above all put on love" is consistent with Paul's more famous passage in 1 Corinthians 13: "the greatest of these is love." Love is the most essential gift we have for doing Christ's work. But Paul listed other qualities that are part of loving. He said to "put on heartfelt compassion, kindness, humility, gentleness, and patience" (v. 12). All of these are part of loving. In fact, in 1 Corinthians 13 Paul listed characteristics of love very similar to these: "Love is patient; love is kind. ... is not boastful; is not conceited [humility]; ... is not provoked [gentleness]." Each characteristic he listed is important to loving in the spirit of Christ.

What six acts or qualities are part of what it means to love?

Heartfelt compassion means going beyond outward acts to opening our heart to another person. Again 1 Corinthians 13:3 says, "And if I donate all my goods to feed the poor, and if I give my body to be burned, but do not have love, I gain nothing." Our giving and loving must be heartfelt rather than a manipulative facade. This is loving in the spirit of Christ. Matthew 9:36 describes Christ's spirit, "When He saw the crowds, He felt compassion for them, because they were weary and worn out, like sheep without a shepherd." We must have the same heartfelt compassion for others going through hard times.

Kindness, listed both here and in 1 Corinthians 13, is often used as a synonym for "mercy." In Micah 6:8 the NRSV says, "What does the Lord require of you but to do justice, and to love kindness, and to walk humbly with your God." The NIV and the King James Version

today's session (cont'd)

translate "mercy" in place of "kindness." Romans 2:4 tells us not to show contempt for God's "kindness" because God's kindness is meant to lead us to repentance. That is also the function of God's mercy.

Humility is sometimes misunderstood in today's world. We think of the self-deprecating person with a terrible self-image who lets him or herself be walked on by others. That is not biblical humility. Jesus Christ himself best defined biblical humility by His own example: "who, existing in the form of God, did not consider equality with God as something to be used for His own advantage. Instead He emptied Himself by assuming the form of a slave, taking on the likeness of men. And when He had come as a man in His external form, He humbled Himself by becoming obedient to the point of death—even to death on a cross" (Phil. 2:6-8). And so humility is being willing to serve others, not because you think you are worthless but because God calls you to help others realize their worth. That is why humility is an important part of loving.

How is a biblical understanding of humility different from the one people often have in the world?

Gentleness means using the kind of tact and sensitivity that acknowledges that human spirits are sometimes easily bruised. Paul reminded the Thessalonians, "instead we were gentle among you, as a nursing mother nurtures her own children" (1 Thess. 2:7). Gentleness is realizing that we are all sometimes as vulnerable as little children.

Patience is what we need to have, realizing that God is not finished with any of us. We are all "works in progress." All of us can look back over our lives and realize that we stand solely on the basis of God's patience with us. We need to show the same kind of patience with each other. Forgiving one another must be part of this patience.

Showing Unity

We were called to Christ not as separate individuals, but as part of one body in Him (v. 15). This is the most common image that Paul used to tell us that we must pull together in unity. When the Corinthian church was breaking apart in schism, Paul told them they could not take communion in a proper spirit "without recognizing the body," that is, if they did not realize their oneness with the other Christians around them (1 Cor. 11:29). He also told them that in a body, all parts need each other and cannot act as if they are independent units (1 Cor. 12). Jesus prayed, "May they all be one, just as You, Father, are in Me and I am in You. May they also be one in Us, so that the world may believe You sent Me" (John 17:21). Without unity among believers, Christ's work suffers.

What is a common image that Paul used to tell Christians that they must act together in unity?

Being Thankful

What two things happen when we decide to live a life of gratitude to God?

The third thing we are to do to glorify Jesus' name is to "be thankful" (v. 15). We are to "do everything in the name of the Lord Jesus, giving thanks to God the Father through Him" (v. 17). Showing this kind of gratitude does two things–it enriches the life of the believer, and it testifies to the goodness of God to nonbelievers. It enriches the life of the believer by making us more aware of the positives in our lives. Some people go through life seeing only the negatives. The story is told of a golfer who had a spirit of negativism. He shot a drive that went off course, ricocheted off a tree, bounced against a rock, and still came to rest on the edge of the green. When his partner asked about his sour, face he responded, "Left myself with a long putt!" How much good needs to happen to us before we recognize it? We can only enjoy the blessings that we recognize are there! An old hymn declares, "Count your many blessings, name them one by one, and it will surprise you what the Lord has done."

Showing thanksgiving also testifies to God's goodness to nonbelievers. People who believe God has given them the short end of the stick are often more than willing to let others know about it. People who recognize God's blessings should also be more than willing to let others know about those blessings and their Source. Sharing your thanksgiving for what God has done for you helps make it possible for God to do the same for another person. As a classic definition of evangelism states, it's "one beggar telling another beggar where to find bread."

notes:

9

Remain in groups of 6–8 people, in a horseshoe configuration.

In this small-group session, students will be applying the lessons of the text to their own lives through the following questions.

The students were asked (in the student book) to choose an answer for each question and explain why.

Learning from the Story (5-7 minutes)

1. What is the relationship between letting the peace of the Messiah rule in your heart and forming the attitudes listed in verses 12 and 13? What do you need to do to open your heart more to this peace?

2. Which of the following comes the closest to the meaning of the phrase, "Let the message about the Messiah dwell richly among you" (v. 16)?
   - ☐ The gospel needs to be lived out in the church, not just taught.
   - ☐ We need to find as many ways as we can to teach about Jesus.
   - ☐ We need to feel the message as well as understand it.
   - ☐ We need to discourage anything that would take our focus off of Christ.

3. What would you say is your biggest barrier to having a consistent attitude of thankfulness?
   - ☐ I have a tendency to see the negative in life.
   - ☐ I don't have much to be thankful for right now.
   - ☐ It isn't the way I was raised.
   - ☐ I'm caught up in our society's drive for more.
   - ☐ I find no barriers—I'm full of thanksgiving right now!
   - ☐ other: ________________________________

notes:

life change lessons (5-7 minutes)

Share with the class the following thoughts on how the lessons of this text might be applied today. The answers to the student book questions (provided in the margin) are underlined unless the question requires a personal answer.

What instances are mentioned that show popular culture's frustration about love and what it means? Can you think of others?

What have Christians already "gotten out" of love?

People have probably felt more frustration with learning how to love than with any other lesson. Romantic love has especially fallen prey to this frustration. A number of years ago Tina Turner sang the popular song *What's Love Got to Do With It?* in which she attempted to take a "sour grapes" approach to love's frustrations. Renee Zellweger took a similar approach in *Down with Love*, a popular movie out much more recently. She played a popular writer advising women to be like men and give up on love while going after sex. Of course, she finds she cannot follow her own advice.

Part of the frustration people have with love is the incredibly heightened expectations of what they are supposed to "get out of it." Today's Scripture has shown us the true issue: how can we *give* in love. It's not that what we get out of it is unimportant; it's just that it is already established. We have received the love and forgiveness of God in Jesus Christ. God has richly blessed us with life in this present world and given us the promise of life beyond this world. What else could He have done to be more loving? Now we are called to show God's love to others. Today's Bible text gets very specific about how we can show this love. Our task is to apply this biblical teaching in our specific life situations.

Here are some suggestions of specific acts for showing this love:

1. DO ONE "SERVANT TASK" AROUND YOUR HOME THAT YOU ARE NOT USED TO DOING. It might be washing the dishes, cleaning toilets, taking out the garbage, vacuuming, or any task you do not normally do. Do this task as often as needed for the rest of the week. Do it without being asked and without pointing out your act for others to notice. Do it simply as an act of humility. If you are used to doing all these things in your home already, go to a rest home, and do a servant act for one of the residents. This can be reading for them, sitting silently with them for an afternoon, adjusting their pillows, or whatever is needed.

2. FORGIVE ONE PERSON YOU HAVE HAD CONFLICT WITH IN THE CHURCH. Pray about this first, and then go to the person and share your desire to forgive them. Do not expect or require that they forgive you back. Do this act solely because God has forgiven you in Jesus Christ.

3. MAKE A LIST OF ALL YOU HAVE TO BE THANKFUL FOR. If you live with other people in a family setting, make this a family project. Post your list in a prominent place, and add to it throughout the week. At the end of one week, get your list and say a prayer of thanks for all of the blessings listed.

CARING TIME
Remain in groups of 6–8 people, in a horseshoe configuration.

Hand out the Prayer/Praise Report to the entire group. Ask each subgroup to pray for the empty chair. Pray specifically for God to guide you to someone to bring next week to fill that chair.

After a sufficient time of prayer in subgroups, close in a corporate prayer. Say, "Next week we will talk about: 'Supreme Submission.' "

Remind participants of the daily Scripture readings and reflective questions found on page 116.

Caring Time (15-20 minutes)

Use this time to pray and care for one another. Today we will begin by sharing things we are thankful for in regard to what has been happening in our group. Take turns having each group member answer the question:

"What has happened in this group for which you are most thankful to God?"

Thank God for all that people share. Then move on to praying for the concerns on the Prayer/Praise Report. Remember to include prayer for the empty chair.

Close by singing a familiar song or chorus of thanks, like the Doxology or "Thank you, Lord."

notes:

BIBLE STUDY NOTES

Reference Notes

Use these notes to gain further understanding of the text as you study on your own.

COLOSSIANS 3:12

God's chosen ones. Christians are heirs to the status of Israel as God's chosen people. But just like with Israel, the Christian is chosen not to special or exclusive privilege, but rather to a mission. Israel was to be "a light to the nations" (Is 49:6). Christians are chosen to spread God's message of love and redemption to all people. As we are told in 1 Peter 2:9, "But you are a chosen race, a royal priesthood, a holy nation, a people for His possession, so that you may proclaim the praises of the One who called you out of darkness into His marvelous light."

COLOSSIANS 3:13

Just as the Lord has forgiven you. Throughout the New Testament, this is the most important motivator for us to forgive others. We find it implicitly in the parable of the Unforgiving Slave (Matt. 18:21-35), in the Lord's Prayer (Matt. 6:9-13), as well as in the teaching of Paul (Eph. 4:32).

COLOSSIANS 3:14

the perfect bond of unity. Laws are sometimes necessary to make people relate to each other responsibly, but laws cannot truly bring us together. Only love, as it has been shown to us in Jesus Christ, can do that.

COLOSSIANS 3:15

And let the peace of the Messiah ... control your hearts. "Your" is plural: What is in view is not just a sense of personal serenity, but a mutual commitment to consider peaceful relationships with one another as the highest priority in their corporate life.

COLOSSIANS 3:16

the message about the Messiah. While the false teachers didn't "hold on to the Head" (2:19), the message the Colossians were to teach one another had to be centered on Jesus.
dwell richly among you. Spiritual fullness is rooted neither in secret knowledge nor in mystical experiences but in a commitment to Christ.
psalms, hymns, and spiritual songs. The psalms refer to the Old Testament Book of Psalms. Hymns were songs common to the church (Luke 1:46-55,68-79; John 1:1-18; Phil. 2:6-11; Rev. 4:8,11). Spiritual songs were spontaneous expressions of praise to Christ.

notes:

Session 10 Supreme Submission

Prepare for the Session

	READINGS	REFLECTIVE QUESTIONS
Monday	Colossians 3:18-19	How difficult is it for you to submit to another person? Can you truly love, or do you get tied up in power struggles?
Tuesday	Colossians 3:20	How do you feel about the way you handled parental authority as a youth? Are you at peace with your parents now? Or are you still rebelling?
Wednesday	Colossians 3:21-22	What are you doing to encourage the children under your care or influence?
Thursday	Luke 2:41-42	What religious traditions are you passing on to your children or the children you influence?
Friday	Luke 2:51-52	What family life memories do you now treasure in your heart?
Saturday	Luke 15:11-32	Are you able to forgive other family members? If not, what holds you back?
Sunday	1 Corinthians 13:4-7	How can you live the standards of 1 Corinthians 13 in your family life today?

OUR GOALS FOR THIS SESSION ARE:

In groups of 6–8, gather people in a horseshoe configuration.

Make sure everyone has a name tag.

Take time to share information on class parties that are coming up as well as any relevant church events.

BIBLE STUDY	• to consider the roles of husband and wife and what it means to "submit" to one another • to understand how abusive or harsh behavior can discourage a spouse or a child • to appreciate the need for personal integrity in both private and public situations
LIFE CHANGE	• to institute the practice of a regular family meeting • to ask one family member to share how our behavior encourages or discourages them • to evaluate how consistent our personal integrity is in private and public situations by keeping a journal of things we do in private that we would not do in public

Icebreaker (10-15 minutes)

INTRODUCE THE ICEBREAKER ACTIVITY: The students have been given instructions in their books.

After the Icebreaker say something like, "While slavery does not officially exist in our country, this does not keep many of us from feeling enslaved, even in our families. Our passage for today talks about slaves but also gives some guidelines for families that can be freeing. These are what we will examine in our session today."

Hand out the Prayer/Praise Report. A sample copy is on pages 166-167. Have people write down prayer requests and praises. Then have the prayer coordinator collect the report and make copies for use during the Caring Time.

Our Emancipation Proclamation. Go around the group on question 1 and let everyone share. Then go around again on questions 2 and 3, as time allows.

1. What is the closest you have come to feeling like a slave?
   - ☐ when I was a kid and had to do what I was told
   - ☐ ever since the honeymoon was over
   - ☐ ever since I've had kids and had to take care of a house
   - ☐ in a former job
   - ☐ in my present job
   - ☐ when I realized how much of my paycheck goes for taxes
   - ☐ other: ________________

2. What do you most feel "enslaved" by right now?
   - ☐ trying to keep up with the bills
   - ☐ my past
   - ☐ trying to maintain a house
   - ☐ an addiction
   - ☐ being a people-pleaser—worrying about what people think
   - ☐ my own workaholic tendencies
   - ☐ the prejudices and stereotypes of society
   - ☐ other: ________________

3. Finish this sentence: "If God would issue me an 'Emancipation Proclamation' He would say ... "

10

notes:

LEARNING FROM THE BIBLE

COLOSSIANS 3:18-22

Have a member of the class, selected ahead of time, read Colossians 3:18-22.

Bible Study (30-45 minutes)

The Scripture for this week:

[18]Wives, be submissive to your husbands, as is fitting in the Lord.
[19]Husbands, love your wives and don't become bitter against them.
[20]Children, obey your parents in everything, for this is pleasing in the Lord.
[21]Fathers, do not exasperate your children, so they won't become discouraged.
[22]Slaves, obey your human masters in everything; don't work only while being watched, in order to please men, but work wholeheartedly, fearing the Lord.

notes:

...about today's session (5 minutes)

Summarize these introductory remarks. Be sure to include the underlined information, which gives the answers to the student book questions (provided in the margin).

What societal problems result from the difficulty people have in walking worthy of the Lord at home?

What person do you know who, like Atticus Finch, is a model of personal integrity?

Why do "false fronts" not work at home?

WHETHER "AT HOME" OR "IN TOWN"

We cannot talk about what it means to walk worthy of the Lord without considering what it means for our family life. It's much easier to put our best foot forward with people we see only occasionally. Behind many a popular public figure there is a "Mommie Dearest" or "Great Santinini" at home. Problems at home then result in crippling societal problems such as child and spousal abuse, divorce, and runaway teens. In the midst of such crises can we give ourselves to the Lord so completely that the people we live with, who know what we are like more than any others, can still see the Lord reflected in our attitudes and behaviors? In today's session we will look at that question.

In the play *To Kill a Mockingbird*, based on the famous book by Harper Lee, Atticus Finch is praised for "being the same at home as he is in town." Perhaps that is why in 2003 the American Film Institute voted Atticus (portrayed in the movie by film legend Gregory Peck) as the greatest movie hero of all time. Being a hero at home cannot be a matter of putting on a false front, since such a facade is bound to slip in one's own home. It has to be a matter of taking on a Christlike spirit. Our text will show us what that means in a concrete way.

notes:

10

Remain in groups of 6–8 people, in a horseshoe configuration.

In this small-group session, students will be responding to the following questions that will help them share their stories in terms of the family life described in Colossians 3:18-22.

Have the students explore these questions together.

Identifying with the Story (5-7 minutes)

1. Which of the following phrases best describes the authority structure in the home where you were raised?
   - ☐ "Father knows best."
   - ☐ "If Mama ain't happy, ain't nobody happy!"
   - ☐ "I'm their leader—which way did they go?"
   - ☐ "Dad wore the pants in the family ... when Mama let him."
   - ☐ "Kids rule!"
   - ☐ Mom and Dad believed in "United we stand; Divided we fall!"

2. In your immediate family, which person would you associate with each of the following words from our text for this week.

   "submissive" ____________________
   "bitter" ____________________
   "pleasing" ____________________
   "discouraged" ____________________

3. What experience did you have as a youth that made you later wish you had obeyed your parent(s)?

notes:

today's session (15-20 minutes)

Share with your class the following information which you may modify according to your own perspectives and teaching needs. The answers to the student book questions (provided in the margin) are underlined.

You might read today's text as a recipe for enslavement. In that spirit certain words and phrases stand out like "be submissive," and "obey ... in everything" (vv. 18,20). This text is often cited legitimating the subjugation of women. Women are put in the same category as children and slaves and are commanded to "do what they are told." To see this passage in such a way is to fail to see it in the context of overall Christian teaching.

Our passage needs to be examined in relation to a central teaching of Jesus. He told the disciples, "The kings of the Gentiles dominate them, and those who have authority over them are called 'Benefactors.' But it must not be like that among you. On the contrary, whoever is greatest among you must become like the youngest, and whoever leads, like the one serving. For who is greater, the one at the table or the one serving? Isn't it the one at the table? But I am among you as the One who serves" (Luke 22:25-27). This puts what Colossians says in a whole different light. Servanthood is not the unique lot of women meant to keep them down, but the calling of every Christian meant to lift us up in identification with our Lord. A parallel passage makes this clearer, calling us to the task of "submitting to one another in the fear of Christ" (Eph.. 5:21). Verse 25 instructs husbands to "love your wives, just as also Christ loved the church and gave Himself for her." To give ourselves up for another is also a form of submission, a form of servanthood.

How does Jesus' teaching about servanthood put Paul's teaching about being submissive in a different light?

This is not to say that husbands and wives will not have duties that are unique to them. It is merely to say we are all called to do certain things to help the family be a freeing, rather than an enslaving, environment. Three guidelines for family life come out of our text today—being submissive, encouraging those we love, and showing integrity.

Being Submissive

In the strictest sense, we are all to submit only to God. Submitting to anyone else when that authority is not acting in line with God's will is wrong. However, Scripture does not allow an attitude of "I defer to God and none other!" Provided they are in accord with God's will, we are to be subject to parents (as children–v. 20) and governing authorities (Rom. 13:1-7). We are also called to submit to one another (Eph.. 5:21). This passage calls wives to be submissive to husbands (v. 18). But all of these subjections are part of our greater subjection to God.

In what four situations does Scripture call us to submit to another person?

To be "submissive" has a connotation for us that confuses the issue somewhat. To us it sounds like a "Stepford Wife" or, even worse, a droopy-tailed dog slumping off under the sofa at his master's displeasure. Other versions use the word "be subject" which sounds

10

today's session (cont'd)

less extreme. To be "subject" means to defer to the will of another. Being submissive requires you to understand that getting what you yourself want must not be your highest value. This understanding is essential if a family is to be strong. Families where the various members are primarily looking for selfish benefits quickly fly apart. Marriages that don't get beyond each partner's "cost-benefit ratio" end with the first stressful times. Traditionally, this role of giving up self for the benefit of family has fallen more on the woman. Some have sought to change this by encouraging married women to think more of self and their own personal goals and ambitions. Our society has painfully found that this only results in more broken families and more insecure children. Certainly women need to have personal goals, and those who love them should encourage those goals. But that does not mean that family should be pushed to second place behind those goals. A better alternative would be to encourage men to see the need to submit themselves to the needs of their family. Men need to give themselves up for their families as Christ gave Himself up for the church (Eph.. 5:25). Doing so will both strengthen families and help men to identify with the servant attitude of Christ. Wherever such a man or woman is, there Christ will be.

What attitude does being "submissive" or "subject" require, and why is this important in a family?

Encouraging Those We Love

Caring for all forms of life requires gentleness. A little seedling must be carefully uprooted when being transplanted. Children must always be taught that baby kittens or puppies should not be squeezed or handled roughly. People are the same. Our spirits are sometimes as fragile as a newborn pup so that they require gentleness. Paul calls husbands to "love your wives and don't become bitter against them" (v. 19). The NIV translates the last part of that verse, "do not be harsh with them," and the NRSV says, "never treat them harshly." In biblical times this was necessary instruction since women were thought of as property, and spousal abuse was often considered a husband's right. Today either party in a marriage may show harshness or acts of bitterness. Such acts include emotional as well as physical harshness. A husband might beat his wife for disagreeing with him. A wife might deride her husband for losing his job. Loving someone means treating that person's spirit like a newly emerged bud of life that must be carefully tended. This doesn't mean we should never challenge our loved ones or be stern with them when such seems to be required. It does mean we should be careful not to crush the spirit of one we love.

Why was the instruction for husbands not to be harsh with their wives especially important in biblical times?

Paul pointed out that what is true of spousal relationships is also true of parent-child relationships, writing "do not exasperate your children, so they won't become discouraged" (v. 21). So with children and spouses we have a choice: we can be a gentle gardener, nurturing life; or we can be like the sheriff in the song *I Shot the Sheriff*. In that song the singer complained of the sheriff, "Every time I planted a seed, he said 'Kill it before it grows.'" Some people are like that. If their child or spouse has a dream, they want to kill it before it grows. The result is bitterness and discouragement in the other person. Hope is one of the most essential elements of life, and discouragement is its enemy. Healthy families nurture hope and avoid whatever might lead to discouragement.

Showing Integrity

Our third guideline is the one that seems less relevant to present day. Paul told slaves to obey their earthly masters. He did so not to support the institution of slavery, but because he felt that was the best way for slaves to witness to their masters. He also wrote something to the slaves that has a bearing on family life and Christian life in general: "don't work only while being watched, in order to please men, but work wholeheartedly, fearing the Lord" (v. 22). This is the principle of showing integrity. We need to teach it to our children. We need to show it to each other. What counts is not what we do when we know we are being watched by the world. What counts is whether or not we hold to our values in the privacy of our homes and even in the inner sanctums of our locked rooms. We need to be the same in our home as we are in public. We need to do all of this because we realize that our true audience—and our true Master—is the Lord Jesus Christ.

Why is it important that a Christian's behavior be consistent at home and in public?

notes:

Remain in groups of 6–8 people, in a horseshoe configuration.

In this small-group session, students will be applying the lessons of the text to their own lives through the following questions.

The students were asked (in the student book) to choose an answer for each question and explain why.

Learning from the Story (5-7 minutes)

1. How does being in the Lord help you in submitting yourself to others?

2. What can you do to be a better encourager, instead of an instrument of discouragement, in your family?
   - ☐ get past my own childhood discouragements
   - ☐ learn to listen better to my family, especially to their feelings and dreams
   - ☐ look for the positive in what people are doing, instead of the negative in what they aren't doing
   - ☐ get my focus off of me
   - ☐ emulate those who have encouraged me
   - ☐ I'm doing this well already.
   - ☐ other: ______________________

3. What is one thing you can do to be more of a person of integrity —to be the same person in your home as you are in public?

notes:

life change lessons (5-7 minutes)

Share with the class the following thoughts on how the lessons of this text might be applied today. The answers to the student book questions (provided in the margin) are underlined unless the question requires a personal answer.

Why is life change in a family system sometimes difficult?

Changing in the context of a family is not always easy. The reason is that a family is a system where everyone finds his or her niche. Each person learns to expect certain behaviors from the other members. They may not like the way the other family members behave, but they adapt to that behavior and to a degree become comfortable with it. When one person starts to change, it disrupts the whole system; and the others are pressured to change as well. That is why family members sometimes sabotage life changes in another family member. For instance, one family member may have a weight problem due to overeating. The person decides to change and go on a diet. No sooner does he or she start to make progress than the other family members start putting tempting food in the way. They "forget" this person is on a diet and make a fancy dessert. Consciously or subconsciously, they are trying to maintain the system and keep the dieter in his or her role as "the fat person." Similarly, even though alcoholism brings a great deal of pain to a family, family members can become anxious when an alcoholic starts to get better. They don't know what this person getting better will do to their role in the family. That is why Alcoholics Anonymous also has groups for family members of alcoholics to help them see their own role in maintaining the alcoholic's sickness and to help them change the whole family system.

What two things are required to change a family system?

Changing a family system therefore requires patience and a willingness to include other family members in talking about changes and why they need to occur. You don't need to ask their permission to change, but it is helpful to give them the chance to think through and express their feelings about what your changes mean to them.

Here are some suggestions for specific acts of life change in relation to family roles:

1. INSTITUTE THE PRACTICE OF A REGULAR FAMILY MEETING. Setting aside a time for this each week is best. Use it as a time to talk about your roles in the family. Evaluate family rules and how well they are being followed. If there is a problem with disobedience, what is that disobedience saying about how the family works? It is often helpful to begin this time with a short devotional or Bible study to help put it all in the context of your faith.

2. ASK ONE FAMILY MEMBER TO SHARE HOW YOUR BEHAVIOR ENCOURAGES OR DISCOURAGES THEM. Just listen to their response. Don't try to defend yourself if something feels like criticism. Hear what the other person has to say. When this person you love has finished, thank him or her for sharing with you. Don't

life change lessons (cont'd)

decide right away how much of what you hear is legitimate. Wait a week! Then evaluate what changes you might make on the basis of what you heard. Sometimes it takes that long for a message to get past our defenses!

3. EVALUATE HOW CONSISTENT YOUR PERSONAL INTEGRITY IS IN PRIVATE AND PUBLIC SITUATIONS BY KEEPING A JOURNAL OF THINGS YOU DO IN PRIVATE THAT YOU WOULD NOT DO IN PUBLIC. Write in the journal each evening, and keep it for at least a week. You don't need to show it to anyone else, unless you choose to show it to a trusted confidant. What does this record say about you? What personal changes does it suggest?

CARING TIME
Remain in groups of 6–8 people, in a horseshoe configuration.

Hand out the Prayer/Praise Report to the entire group. Ask each subgroup to pray for the empty chair. Pray specifically for God to guide you to someone to bring next week to fill that chair.

After a sufficient time of prayer in subgroups, close in a corporate prayer. Say, "Next week we will talk about: 'Service with a Smile.' "

Remind participants of the daily Scripture readings and reflective questions found on page 128.

Caring Time (15-20 minutes)

Close by sharing prayer requests and praying for one another, especially for family members who are in need. Begin by having each group member answer the question:

"What person in your family, immediate or extended, especially needs the prayers of this group right now?"

Pray for the concerns that people share. Then move on to praying for the concerns on the Prayer/Praise Report. Continue to pray for God to guide you to someone to bring next week to fill the empty chair.

notes:

BIBLE STUDY NOTES

Reference Notes

Use these notes to gain further understanding of the text as you study on your own.

COLOSSIANS 3:18

be submissive. In Christ, this is transformed from a passive obedience to an authority to a specific application of Christ's call to put the needs and interest of others before one's own (Eph. 5:21-24; Phil. 2:4).

COLOSSIANS 3:19

love. This is the distinctively Christian *agape* love involving the willful decision to do good for another regardless of personal cost.

COLOSSIANS 3:20

obey your parents. See Exodus 20:12.

COLOSSIANS 3:21

Fathers. This word can mean "parents" as well (Heb. 11:23).

COLOSSIANS 3:22

Slaves. Slaves were legally considered the property of their masters. While obedience was required at the threat of punishment, Paul called for an attitude of faithful service in light of the fact that, ultimately, Christ is the master of all.

notes:

Session

11

Service with a Smile

Prepare for the Session

	READINGS	REFLECTIVE QUESTIONS
Monday	Colossians 3:23	How enthusiastic are you about your faith? Have you lost the spark?
Tuesday	Colossians 3:24	How confident do you feel of the inheritance waiting for you in heaven? What could help you feel more assured by this promise?
Wednesday	Colossians 3:25–4:1	Do you sometimes envy a person with a sinful lifestyle? Are you doing all you can to witness to such people and encourage them to change?
Thursday	Nehemiah 8:5-12	Have you ever been so touched by the promises of Scripture that you were moved to tears? Are you letting Scripture truly touch your heart?
Friday	Acts 2:42-47	Are you participating in a fellowship that is full of enthusiasm and joy? What can you do to make your church more loving and joyful?
Saturday	Acts 5:41-42	Does the prospect of having to make sacrifices for Christ scare you or help you to feel "part of the team"?
Sunday	Philippians 4:4-7	Do you rejoice over what God has done or complain about what is *not* happening? How can you change that attitude?

OUR GOALS FOR THIS SESSION ARE:

In groups of 6–8, gather people in a horseshoe configuration.

Make sure everyone has a name tag.

Take time to share information on class parties that are coming up as well as any relevant church events.

BIBLE STUDY
- to consider what it means to work for the Lord with enthusiasm, and to see what can interfere with that enthusiasm
- to realize the difference between doing work to please the Lord and doing work to please people
- to be reminded of the reward we are promised in Jesus Christ, and to hold the promise of that reward before us

LIFE CHANGE
- to continue to explore any spiritual discouragements or questions we have
- to dedicate each ministry or service we are involved in to the Lord
- to post God's promises in our home

Icebreaker (10-15 minutes)

INTRODUCE THE ICEBREAKER ACTIVITY: The students have been given instructions in their books.

After the Icebreaker say something like, "Enthusiasm is not something we can have just because we are 'supposed to.' However, today's text tells us that a life in Christ will have true enthusiasm in serving Him. As we look at this passage we will learn what that means."

Hand out the Prayer/Praise Report. A sample copy is on pages 166-167. Have people write down prayer requests and praises. Then have the prayer coordinator collect the report and make copies for use during the Caring Time.

Getting "Pumped." Go around the group on question 1 and let everyone share. Then go around again on questions 2 and 3, as time allows.

1. When are you most likely to get really "pumped" about something?

   ☐ when my favorite sports team is winning
   ☐ when there is a sale at my favorite store
   ☐ when the stock market is up
   ☐ when it's a beautiful day and I have time off
   ☐ when I get a visit from old friends
   ☐ when I am caught up in an exciting project
   ☐ when I'm at a concert by my favorite group or singer
   ☐ when I get to see my grandchildren
   ☐ when my children are honored for an achievement
   ☐ other: ______________________________

2. How can other people tell when you're really enthusiastic or excited about something?

   ☐ I'm hyper! ☐ I'm like a kid! ☐ I say "Yippie!"
   ☐ I move more quickly and smile a lot!
   ☐ The corners of my mouth turn up ... a little.
   ☐ I doubt if they can tell.
   ☐ I'm not sure *I* can tell!

Icebreaker (cont'd)

3. Finish this sentence: "The most enthusiasm I felt in church or in doing something for God was when..."

notes:

LEARNING FROM THE BIBLE

COLOSSIANS 3:23–4:1

Have a member of the class, selected ahead of time, read Colossians 3:23–4:1

Bible Study (30-45 minutes)

The Scripture for this week:

[23]Whatever you do, do it enthusiastically, as something done for the Lord and not for men, [24]knowing that you will receive the reward of an inheritance from the Lord—you serve the Lord Christ. [25]For the wrongdoer will be paid back for whatever wrong he has done, and there is no favoritism.

[1]Masters, supply your slaves with what is right and fair, since you know that you too have a Master in heaven.

notes:

Summarize these introductory remarks. Be sure to include the underlined information, which gives the answers to the student book questions (provided in the margin).

...about today's session (5 minutes)

TO HAVE GOD WITHIN US

The word "enthusiasm" comes from the Greek words *en theos*, which mean "in God." To have enthusiasm is to have the spirit of God within us! How different the church might be if we really lived out that definition. How much "enthusiasm" do we show as Christians? Somewhat of a rift exists in the church between those designated as "charismatic" and those who would resist such a designation for themselves. Charismatics sometimes deride non-charismatics as lacking enthusiasm. However, enthusiasm is not a matter of worship style. Enthusiasm is a matter of the energy with which we do the work of Christ. One can be emotionally expressive in worship and yet show little enthusiasm for working for the Lord. In a similar vein, one can have a quiet, meditative worship style and be a ball of fire in working for the Lord. The Bible tells us, "Whatever you do, do it enthusiastically" (3:23). Whatever we do, we are to do with energy and the spirit of God within us.

What Greek words does the word "enthusiasm" come from? What does it mean?

What would you say is the relationship between worship style and showing enthusiasm in your service to the Lord?

The question Christians need to face is: "Why don't more Christians feel enthusiastic about their faith?" Winning sports teams generally get enthusiasm from their fans without having to ask for it—although a chant encouraged by the organ and words on the Jumbo-Tron does sometimes give fans an extra nudge! Singing stars may even have to "dial down" the enthusiasm of some of their fans—like when they start breaking down barriers and crawling up on stage. Delegates at a political convention may have some of their enthusiasm orchestrated, but many are "true believers" as is evident by the waving signs and pressing throngs of people.

Part of the reason sports and entertainment fans show more enthusiasm than Christians may be because they have the object of their enthusiasm in clear view, right in front of them. Ours is less visible. Still, Christians can and sometimes do evidence a real enthusiasm for the Lord in what they do. In our session today we want to take a look at how that can be encouraged and increased.

What reason is mentioned for why sports and entertainment fans often show more enthusiasm than Christians do for Christ? What do you think about this?

notes:

Remain in groups of 6–8 people, in a horseshoe configuration.

In this small-group session, students will be responding to the following questions that will help them share their stories in terms of serving the Lord enthusiastically as Colossians 3:23–4:1 teaches.

Have the students explore these questions together.

Identifying with the Story (5-7 minutes)

1. Did favoritism play a role in the family in which you were raised? How was it expressed? How did you respond?

2. In the work that you do, whether paid, volunteer, or at home, whom are you most working to please?

   - ☐ A parent—I still live by their standards.
   - ☐ My spouse—I want him/her to approve of what I do.
   - ☐ My children—I want them to think I'm a good parent.
   - ☐ My boss—I respect his/her opinion.
   - ☐ Myself—I have my own high standards.
   - ☐ My friends—I want to impress them with my skill and success.
   - ☐ In all honesty, the Lord.
   - ☐ other: ____________________

3. Of all the things you are called upon to do for the Lord, which one do you have the hardest time doing enthusiastically?

   - ☐ studying the Bible
   - ☐ worshiping
   - ☐ sharing my faith with others
   - ☐ giving money
   - ☐ helping people in need
   - ☐ other: ____________
   - ☐ serving on church boards or committees

notes:

today's session (15-20 minutes)

Share with your class the following information which you may modify according to your own perspectives and teaching needs. The answers to the student book questions (provided in the margin) are underlined.

If you ask a football coach how to build enthusiasm for his team, he might simply say, "Have a winning team, and get good cheerleaders." If you ask a political candidate how to build enthusiasm, he or she might refer to getting a good press agent and lining up lots of photo ops. If you ask a singer in a band the same question, the response you get might include references to a hot venue and good front people. But what do we do to get people to increase their enthusiasm for working for the Lord? There are no magical answers, but Scripture does give us a couple of hints.

Focus on Christ, not People

What group did Paul primarily address in this text?

In our text Paul wrote primarily to Christian slaves. Nevertheless, his message can apply to all people seeking to do work that is pleasing to the Lord: "Whatever you do, do it enthusiastically, as something done for the Lord and not for men" (3:23). He also called masters to act mindful of the fact that they also have a Master—in heaven.

What four examples are given of people working in ministries to please people and not God? Can you think of others?

Much work, even work in the church or in ministering organizations, is in reality done to please people. We want the other people in the church to think of us as righteous or dedicated or creative or intelligent. The soloist who gets jealous over another soloist is seeking to please people. For someone seeking to please the Lord, the presence of another talented soloist would be a source of joy since it would bring more glory to God. The pastor who does not confront a disruptive member is seeking to please people, not God. A pastor seeking to please God would regard the effective functioning of Christ's church as more important than whether a disruptive member gets mad at him or her. Donors who insist on having their name on a plaque or even on a church building are seeking to be seen by people and are not seeking to please the Lord. The person who stops ministering to the poor because some of the people who received help "did not seem grateful" is in reality working to please people. If we are working to please Christ, whether or not certain people are grateful is irrelevant.

List two ways working to please people rather than God is detrimental?

We are not supposed to disregard totally what other people think. God created us as social creatures. That means what others think of us will have some level of importance. However, if others' opinions become very high in importance to us, we are doing two detrimental things. First, we are acting counter to our call to put Christ first. Nothing can be more important to us than pleasing Christ. Second, we are setting ourselves up for frustration. A well-known saying warns, "You can please all of the people some of the time, and some of the people all of the time; but you cannot please all of the people

today's session (cont'd)

all of the time." Those who try to do so will soon grow discouraged. How can we be enthusiastic if we keep setting ourselves up for this kind of discouragement? If we are seeking to please Christ, we will not become discouraged when some people are ungrateful, or some church leaders don't appreciate us, or some other church leaders seem to be in it for themselves. We will not be focusing on or seeking their pleasure.

We will not be frustrated if we focus on Christ while we are serving Him and others. He always sees and appreciates. Christ warns us, "Be careful not to practice your righteousness in front of people, to be seen by them. Otherwise, you will have no reward from your Father in heaven. So whenever you give to the poor, don't sound a trumpet before you, as the hypocrites do in the synagogues and on the streets, to be applauded by people. I assure you: They've got their reward! But when you give to the poor, don't let your left hand know what your right hand is doing, so that your giving may be in secret. And your Father who sees in secret will reward you" (Matt. 6:1-4).

Serving Christ enthusiastically can be done more easily if we don't corrupt the process by trying to please people. The satisfaction that comes from pleasing Christ will be its own reward and will build our enthusiasm instead of our discouragement.

Remember Our True Reward

Part of what can build our enthusiasm is remembering our true reward. When we focus on people, we focus on earthly rewards: human praise and fame, business connections, perhaps sexual attention. These rewards are at best fleeting. We should work "knowing that you will receive the reward of an inheritance from the Lord" (3:24). Thus, in addition to pleasing Christ, we have the reward of eternal life with Christ along with our loved ones in Him. This is a reward that Christ compared to great treasures: "The kingdom of heaven is like treasure, buried in a field, that a man found and reburied. Then in his joy he goes and sells everything he has and buys that field. Again, the kingdom of heaven is like a merchant in search of fine pearls. When he found one priceless pearl, he went and sold everything he had, and bought it" (Matt. 13:44-46). Note the enthusiasm of those finding the treasures. We are told that "in his joy" he sold everything he had! He didn't decide regretfully to make this "sacrifice." In his joy he gave up everything for a reward he was confident was worth it. <u>That is the important factor—confidence the reward will be worth it.</u>

What is the most important factor in determining whether a reward will make us enthusiastic for our work?

The rewards of this world do not always come through for us. We can work for years trying to earn a promotion, only to have that promotion end up going to a rival who had an in with the boss. We can build up our financial fortune, only to have it lost in a stock market crash, law suit, or uninsured loss. For every person the world defines as successful, at least 10 more struggle along in frustration. Even the one defined as successful sometimes looks around and wonders if it was worth it. When John D. Rockefeller was asked how much money it takes to satisfy a person, he said, "Just a little more!"

What rewards do we have or will we receive for working for Christ?

We can be confident the reward of God's kingdom will be worth it. Not only will we live eternally with Christ, but the relationships we begin in this life will never have to end if they are in Christ (1 Thess. 4:13-18). That is why we can work toward God's promises with enthusiasm. Hebrews 6:17-19 promises us, "Because God wanted to show His unchangeable purpose even more clearly to the heirs of the promise, He guaranteed it with an oath, so that through two unchangeable things, in which it is impossible for God to lie, we who have fled for refuge might have strong encouragement to seize the hope set before us. We have this hope—like a sure and firm anchor of the soul." Our reward is as sure as the promises of God, and that makes it worthy of our enthusiasm.

notes:

Remain in groups of 6–8 people, in a horseshoe configuration.

In this small-group session, students will be applying the lessons of the text to their own lives through the following questions.

The students were asked (in the student book) to choose an answer for each question and explain why.

Learning from the Story (5-7 minutes)

1. What is currently limiting your enthusiasm for the Lord?
   - ☐ the hypocrisy and political maneuvering I see in the church
   - ☐ the distractions of the world
   - ☐ some spiritually discouraging experiences I have had of late (like the death of a loved one)
   - ☐ my cynicism about the Lord's promises
   - ☐ the wrongdoers I see apparently prospering
   - ☐ Nothing—I'm really "pumped"!
   - ☐ other: ____________________

2. How do you feel about the wrongdoers you see in the world?
   - ☐ Sometimes I feel a little envious of what they get away with.
   - ☐ "Been there. Done that. Bought the t-shirt. Ready to move on."
   - ☐ I feel sorry for them. They're heading in the wrong direction.
   - ☐ I feel sorry for them—God will punish them.
   - ☐ I'm kind of looking forward to God punishing them.
   - ☐ I feel frustrated I haven't been able to do more to get through to them.
   - ☐ other: ____________________

3. What most fans the flames of your enthusiasm for Christ?
   - ☐ the other enthusiastic Christians I meet
   - ☐ the worship services I attend
   - ☐ my own private devotional time
   - ☐ seeing what Christians are doing for good in the world
   - ☐ reading the promises of God in Scripture

notes:

Share with the class the following thoughts on how the lessons of this text might be applied today. The answers to the student book questions (provided in the margin) are underlined unless the question requires a personal answer.

What are three things that can block a person's enthusiasm for a good work?

What is the best approach to dealing with unresolved anger at God or spiritual questions?

life change lessons (5-7 minutes)

Three things can block a person's enthusiasm for a good work: wrong expectations, unresolved anger or questions, and lack of awareness of the work's potential. In relation to working for Christ's kingdom, we have sought to address all three of these in this session. A wrong expectation is that we can please people. We have seen how trying to do that leads to frustration. Unresolved anger or questions can include cynicism about God's promises that one has not had the courage to talk about or being angry about a spiritually discouraging experience. An example of the latter is when a person loses a loved one to tragic death and feels angry at God about it. You can try to hide your feelings about this, but it will surely dampen your enthusiasm for the Lord! The best approach is to talk about it in all honesty with other Christian friends. That is what we have sought to encourage in some of our questions. An unresolved cynicism is the same. A person needs to talk about it in honesty.

A third enthusiasm blocker is lack of awareness of the potential of what God promises us. We have tried in today's session to help all of us have a greater awareness of what God promises us in eternal life. It is a sure promise worthy of our enthusiasm. Now we need to make some life changes that will bring a greater enthusiasm for the Lord. Here are some suggestions:

1. CONTINUE TO EXPLORE ANY SPIRITUAL DISCOURAGEMENTS OR QUESTIONS YOU HAVE. Get together with someone in this group or another Christian friend to continue discussing your feelings about lost loved ones or spiritual trauma that has brought unresolved questions. Include in these get-togethers prayer for your healing.

2. DEDICATE EACH MINISTRY OR SERVICE YOU ARE INVOLVED IN TO THE LORD. Before each committee meeting, leadership assignment, or ministry involvement, dedicate what you do to the Lord. Say a prayer like this: "Lord, all I do here is for you. Help me to remain focused on that, and I will give you the praise." This will remind you not to get tied up in issues of what other people think or appreciate. Do this for several weeks, and see what difference it makes in your attitude.

3. POST GOD'S PROMISES IN YOUR HOME. Have a place on your refrigerator or in your room to post God's promises that are most important to you. You might begin with some included in this lesson. Every time you hear or read a promise that speaks to you, add it to your list. When you pass by the list, read these promises over to remind you of the purpose and eternal reward of your work and life.

CARING TIME
Remain in groups of 6–8 people, in a horseshoe configuration.

Hand out the Prayer/ Praise Report to the entire group. Ask each subgroup to pray for the empty chair. Pray specifically for God to guide you to someone to bring next week to fill that chair.

After a sufficient time of prayer in subgroups, close in a corporate prayer. Say, "Next week we will talk about: 'Seeker Salt.' "

Remind participants of the daily Scripture readings and reflective questions found on page 140.

Caring Time (15-20 minutes)

During this time, have everyone in the group share prayer requests and pray for one another. Today, let us especially pray for any spiritual wounds group members may have. Begin by having each member answer the question:

"What spiritual wound have you experienced (a death, a disappointment, etc.) for which you need prayer support right now?"

Pray for the wounds that people share and that God would give them healing, peace, and strength. In addition, pray for the concerns on the Prayer/Praise Report.

notes:

BIBLE STUDY NOTES

Reference Notes

Use these notes to gain further understanding of the text as you study on your own.

COLOSSIANS 3:24

inheritance. The Christian looks forward to inheriting the fullness of the kingdom of God (Luke 12:32; Eph. 5:5). This hope (1:5) provides the basis for "endurance and patience" with thanksgiving (1:11-12), even in the types of hardships a slave might face.

COLOSSIANS 3:25

For the wrongdoer will be paid back for whatever wrong he has done. Whereas in Ephesians 6:8, Paul promised slaves that "the Lord will reward everyone for whatever good he does," here he warned that misbehavior will result in judgment.

there is no favoritism. Slaves, even though oppressed by their masters, cannot expect God to excuse sin (v. 22). Ephesians 6:9 applies this same phrase to masters, warning them that their position of authority will not exempt them from judgment should they abuse that authority.

COLOSSIANS 4:1

supply your slaves with what is right and fair. While Paul did not oppose slavery as such, he did call upon Christian masters to treat their slaves with justice and consideration, values which Roman law did not require of them.

you too have a Master in heaven. Masters are to relate to their slaves in the full realization that God is their Master and they are accountable to Him for their behavior toward their slaves.

notes:

Session

12

Seeker Salt

Prepare for the Session

	READINGS	REFLECTIVE QUESTIONS
Monday	Colossians 4:2	Are you able to maintain a regular, consistent prayer life?How can you be better disciplined in this area?
Tuesday	Colossians 4:3-4	When you tell friends you will pray for them, do you follow through with your promise? Why or why not?
Wednesday	Colossians 4:5	Are you reaching out to outsiders and non-Christians, or are you pulling back into the safety of familiar people who already believe?
Thursday	Colossians 4:6	Do you frequently find that you are wishing you could take back things that you said? What can you do to speak with more discipline and love?
Friday	James 5:13-16	How confident are you in the effectiveness of prayer? Do you show in your actions that you believe it can make a difference?
Saturday	James 5:19-20	What are you doing to help nonbelievers find the grace of God in Jesus Christ?
Sunday	James 3:12-13	What can you do to make your tongue more of an instrument of love and less one of destruction?

OUR GOALS FOR THIS SESSION ARE:

In groups of 6–8, gather people in a horseshoe configuration.

Make sure everyone has a name tag.

Take time to share information on class parties that are coming up as well as any relevant church events.

INTRODUCE THE ICEBREAKER ACTIVITY: The students have been given instructions in their books.

After the Icebreaker say something like, "Paul was familiar with open and closed doors. When the doors for preaching closed in the provinces of Asia and Bithynia, Paul had a vision that swung a door wide open in Macedonia. In today's text he asked the Christians at Colossae to pray that God would once again open such a door. Today we will consider asking for open doors as one of the functions of prayer."

Hand out the Prayer/Praise Report. A sample copy is on pages 166-167. Have people write down prayer requests and praises. Then have the prayer coordinator collect the report and make copies for use during the Caring Time.

BIBLE STUDY
- to look at the importance of prayer in opening doors between nonbelievers and Jesus Christ
- to consider how we can relate to nonbelievers with wisdom
- to learn what it means for our speech to be "gracious" and to discover how to manifest such speech to nonbelievers

LIFE CHANGE
- to develop and maintain a prayer list of people who need to open their heart to Jesus
- to meet someone who is not a Christian and learn three interesting facts about that person
- to have a trusted friend help us evaluate how we speak to strangers

Icebreaker (10-15 minutes)

Open Doors. Go around the group on question 1 and let everyone share. Then go around again on questions 2 and 3, as time allows.

1. To which of the following would you most like to have an "open door" anytime you wished to enter?

☐ Madison Square Garden
☐ the Oval Office
☐ The Smithsonian Institute
☐ Disney World
☐ the locker room of my favorite sports team
☐ the floor of the New York Stock Exchange
☐ my favorite celebrity's wardrobe
☐ the conference room of a business rival
☐ other: ____________________

2. In which of the following situations in your life do you feel you have an open door (no big barriers and/or lots of opportunity)? In which of them do you feel the "door" is closed (communication is shut down, opportunities are few)? Write by each one either "O" for open or "C" for closed.

____ your marriage or most intimate relationship
____ your profession
____ your relationship with your children
____ your relationship to God
____ your future in general

12

Icebreaker (cont'd)

3. Finish this sentence: "The door I would like to see open for our class or group would be the door to ..."

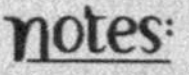

LEARNING FROM THE BIBLE

COLOSSIANS 4:2-6

Have a member of the class, selected ahead of time, read Colossians 4:2-6.

Bible Study (30-45 minutes)

The Scripture for this week:

2Devote yourselves to prayer; stay alert in it with thanksgiving. 3At the same time, pray also for us that God may open a door to us for the message, to speak the mystery of the Messiah—for which I am in prison— 4so that I may reveal it as I am required to speak. 5Walk in wisdom toward outsiders, making the most of the time. 6Your speech should always be gracious, seasoned with salt, so that you may know how you should answer each person.

notes:

Summarize these introductory remarks. Be sure to include the underlined information, which gives the answers to the student book questions (provided in the margin).

...about today's session (5 minutes)

A CLOSED-DOOR POLICY

An open door is a rarity in modern crime-conscious America. When America was largely rural, people used to keep doors unlocked and even standing open. Neighbors were encouraged to stop by without even calling ahead (most didn't have phones!), and in some places coming in without knocking was common. Today, however, doors are often double-locked and armed with security systems. Neighbors not only don't drop by; they often don't even know each other. Apartment buildings in many settings restrict entry even into the outside halls, and you have to know a code or call ahead to get in. Modern America is rapidly developing a "closed-door policy."

The closed doors of our buildings are symbolic of a bigger problem—the closed doors to our spirit. We don't let others in to see who we are or to truly touch our soul. We put in so much effort to protect ourselves from each other that we end up feeling isolated and alone. When we do try to connect with each other, it's through the Internet. The Internet flourishes because it offers a degree of anonymity and allows communication between people who might not otherwise connect with each other. <u>However, the connections lack the personal warmth of face-to-face encounter, and the anonymity sometimes only offers "protection" for those with destructive motives, like child molesters and scam artists.</u> The Internet then may be opening doors for such abuses while not truly opening doors to real relationship.

What are two drawbacks of the Internet in relation to opening doors to others?

In seeking to spread the gospel of Jesus Christ, Paul was interested in what would open doors. He wanted to open doors to people who could then experience the life-transforming power of Jesus Christ. In his world people also wanted to protect themselves, and doors would sometimes become closed. <u>They were often closed by the religious leaders who wanted to protect what they perceived to be their monopoly on truth. Sometimes they were closed by the political leaders in Rome who wanted to preserve their political power from anyone who spoke of another "kingdom."</u>

What two groups closed doors to Paul in his time?

In today's text Paul sought to enlist the Christians in Colossae to assist him in opening doors. <u>He mentions three actions by which they could help—praying, walking in wisdom, and manifesting gracious speech.</u> We want to take a look at how we can also use these tools to open doors to relationships in Christ.

What were three actions Paul suggested to the Colossians for helping to open doors for Christ?

Remain in groups of 6–8 people, in a horseshoe configuration.

In this small-group session, students will be responding to the following questions that will help them share their stories in terms of Paul's direction in Colossians 4:2-6.

Have the students explore these questions together.

Identifying with the Story (5-7 minutes)

1. In the course of your lifetime, whom have you most often seen as "outsiders"?
   - ☐ people from other parts of the country ("Yankees," New Yorkers, Californians, etc.)
   - ☐ agitators for a minority political cause
   - ☐ people of other races
   - ☐ foreigners
   - ☐ farmers and country people
   - ☐ homeless people
   - ☐ people with addictions
   - ☐ non-Christians
   - ☐ me
   - ☐ other: ______________

2. What would you say is the biggest or most noticeable barrier between you and the outsider group you mentioned in question 1 (or between you and others if your response was "me")?
   - ☐ the demands they make on me and my culture
   - ☐ the way they talk
   - ☐ the way they dress
   - ☐ just different life experiences
   - ☐ the way they think
   - ☐ different values and beliefs
   - ☐ other: ______________

3. What have you found to be most effective in opening doors with the outsider group you mentioned in question 1?
   - ☐ plain old talking and listening
   - ☐ finding shared interests—a common value or cause
   - ☐ finding shared interests—like in sports, the arts, or music
   - ☐ praying and worshiping with them
   - ☐ taking the risk of reaching out
   - ☐ working on projects where we have a common interest
   - ☐ I have never tried
   - ☐ other: ______________________________

notes:

today's session (15-20 minutes)

Share with your class the following information which you may modify according to your own perspectives and teaching needs. The answers to the student book questions (provided in the margin) are underlined.

How was Paul's view on "outsiders" different than that of the traditional Jew of the time?

In a sense, Paul believed in a Christian church with no outsiders. In Galatians 3:28 he wrote, "There is no Jew or Greek, slave or free, male or female; for you are all one in Christ Jesus." He lived in a world where the traditional Jew believed that all Gentiles were outsiders by virtue of birth. Paul rejected this interpretation when he took the gospel to Gentiles. However, people could choose to exclude themselves by rejecting Christ. Paul referred to these "self-excluders" with the word "outsiders."

In Paul's day why didn't Christians think of themselves as "outsiders," even though they had reason to?

Significantly, Christians did not think of *themselves* as outsiders. The rest of the world did. Christians didn't go along with the multiplicity of gods worshiped in Roman society, but neither did they any longer fit in with the traditional Jewish communities who rejected Jesus. In fact, more and more they were being kicked out of the synagogues. In terms of numbers, even with their fantastic growth rate, they were still a small minority. Still Christians didn't think of themselves as outsiders because they belonged to a different kind of kingdom, a different kind of society. We learn from 1 Peter 2:9, "But you are a chosen race, a royal priesthood, a holy nation, a people for His possession." That is the really important group to belong to; those who don't are the true outsiders.

Christians are not to be smug in their status, however. They are to find ways to open doors for outsiders to be part of who they are. Paul gave some directions on how to do this. He called on Christians to pray that doors would be opened, to show wisdom in relating to outsiders, and to speak graciously. Let's look at how each of these is important.

Praying for Open Doors

Paul invited the Colossians to "Devote yourselves to prayer" (v. 2) and more specifically to "pray also for us that God may open a door to us for the message" (v. 3). Jesus had told His disciples from the first that prayer would be an important tool in helping them do the mission He was giving them. After demonstrating His power by causing a fig tree to wither, He promised, " I assure you: If you have faith and do not doubt, you will not only do what was done to the fig tree, but even if you tell this mountain, 'Be lifted up and thrown into the sea,' it will be done. And everything–whatever you ask in prayer, believing–you will receive" (Matt. 21:21-22). This power was not promised to the disciples so they could gain material benefit, but so they could effectively minister in Jesus' name.

What four positive results had the church already experienced from the power of prayer before Paul wrote these words?

By the time Paul wrote the words in this passage, prayer had already resulted in Peter's miraculous escape from prison (Acts 12:1-17), the beginning of the mission to the Gentiles by Paul and Barnabas

today's session (cont'd)

(Acts 13:1-3), an open door for that mission into Europe (Acts 16:6-10), and a deliverance of Paul and Silas from prison (Acts 16:16-40). This list includes only the most obvious instances. Because of such events, Paul and his team had learned to believe in the power of prayer.

Now Paul was praying for another open door for his ministry. We don't know if he was particularly asking because he had been meeting some closed doors, but we know he asked believing in the power of prayer to make a difference. God continued to open doors for Paul right to the end of his ministry as he witnessed to the Roman soldiers who guarded him in prison, wrote his well-known letters, and perhaps even took the gospel to Spain.

Prayer is an essential tool for us to open doors to ministering to those outside of the faith. People put up a variety of barriers to close the door to their spirit—defensiveness, cynicism, intellectualism, and personal isolationism. Prayer helps us get past these barriers others put up, and it draws on the power of the Holy Spirit to change human hearts. Paul's heart was hardened when he was persecuting the church. The Holy Spirit changed him, and his story helps us to learn that the Holy Spirit can change anyone.

Relating to Outsiders with Wisdom

List three possible, but somewhat deficient, ways of relating to outsiders.

Paul gave the Colossians a second instruction, "Walk in wisdom toward outsiders, making the most of the time" (v. 5). This would also help open the doors of witness. A Christian can take a variety of approaches to those outside of the faith, but several of them can hinder witness. That is why wisdom is needed. One approach is the self-righteous approach. Too many people feel Christians come at them from this perspective. "We are better than you are" is the message they hear. This is actually the approach the Pharisees used with Jesus. It didn't work then, and it doesn't work now.

A second approach people use is avoidance. The idea here is to not be "polluted" by the wrong thinking and bad behavior of the nonbeliever. In Old Testament times Israel often used this approach, and it carried over somewhat with the Jews of Jesus' time. This approach certainly contains some truth. The old saying is "Bad company ruins good morals." However, not all nonbelievers have bad morals, and you can't really touch the life of someone for Jesus Christ if you avoid a real relationship with them.

A third approach is "blending in." The idea here is to become like the nonbeliever—to value what they value, to laugh at what they laugh at, to go to the same parties they go to, and to accept their culture. Again some truth appears in this approach. Paul declared himself willing to change according to his cultural environment: "To the Jews I became like a Jew, to win Jews; to those under the law, like one under the law–though I myself am not under the law –to win those under the law. To those who are outside the law, like one outside the law–not being outside God's law, but under the law of Christ–to win those outside the law. To the weak I became weak, in order to win the weak. I have become all things to all people, so that I may by all means save some" (1 Cor. 9:20-22). The problem with this approach is that one can become so much like the nonbeliever that the "Christian's" life no longer bears witness for the difference Christ makes. The contemporary culture is not challenged by the high standards of Jesus Christ.

The deficiency of these other approaches makes a fourth one necessary: relating to those outside the faith with wisdom. This means knowing when to "blend in" and when not to conform. It means knowing when to move closer to a person and show concern and when to pull back. It means knowing when to be different and when to point out how many ways we are all the same. Jesus told his followers, "Look, I'm sending you out like sheep among wolves. Therefore be as shrewd as serpents and harmless as doves" (Matt. 10:16). This is the same approach Paul was advocating to open doors among nonbelievers.

Speaking Graciously

Finally Paul told the Colossians, "Your speech should always be gracious, seasoned with salt, so that you may know how you should answer each person" (v. 6). "Gracious" speech is speech that conveys God's grace, God's unmerited favor. If we want to open doors to nonbelievers, our speech should not be contentious, judgmental, negative, or harsh. Rather it should convey God's grace, mercy, and love. It should be "seasoned with salt." This reminds us that Christ calls us to be "the salt of the earth" (Matt. 5:13). Salt was used in ancient times to both flavor and preserve food. Jesus wants us to flavor the world with God's love and to preserve that which is valuable in life from the spoilage of sin and hate. Our speech should be a positive influence in this way. When it is, it will open doors for people seeking the way of God.

What did Paul mean by having speech "seasoned with salt" (v. 6)?

notes:

Remain in groups of 6–8 people, in a horseshoe configuration.

In this small-group session, students will be applying the lessons of the text to their own lives through the following questions.

The students were asked (in the student book) to choose an answer for each question and explain why.

Learning from the Story (5-7 minutes)

1. What is God calling you to do to better reach out to those outside the faith?
   - ☐ to stop being so protective of myself and to take risks
   - ☐ to keep this need in my prayers
   - ☐ to listen to nonbelievers more
   - ☐ to have more courage in saying what I believe
   - ☐ to learn to speak more positively
   - ☐ to move out of my small circle of friends
   - ☐ other: ____________________

2. Which of the following do you think is most important for speech to be gracious?
   - ☐ having a gentle tone
   - ☐ avoiding negative or judgmental statements
   - ☐ referring often to Christ and God's love
   - ☐ affirming the person with whom you are talking
   - ☐ being honest and sincere
   - ☐ avoiding sarcasm and inflammatory statements

3. How would you say you are doing in the area of showing "gracious" speech?
   - ☐ Great—my words are as sweet as honey.
   - ☐ Well, SOME of them are as honey ... overall, more like sweet and sour sauce.
   - ☐ My speech can be gracious when I set my mind to it.
   - ☐ My speech has some pretty rough edges.
   - ☐ I tell it like it is ... and sometimes that's not very pretty!
   - ☐ other: ____________________

notes:

Share with the class the following thoughts on how the lessons of this text might be applied today. The answers to the student book questions (provided in the margin) are underlined unless the question requires a personal answer.

life change lessons (5-7 minutes)

People used to knock on a lot more doors in this country. Neighborhood children used to knock on the door to ask a child to play. Now they instant message or text message them. Door-to-door salesmen used to frequent every neighborhood. Now they call on the phone (usually at dinner time!), or they send you a pop up message on your computer screen. Church members used to knock on a lot of doors as a form of outreach. While that still happens, now more send out mass mailings.

There is a sense in which we will always be having to knock on closed doors—we will be forever having to knock on the personal doors people have closed to Jesus Christ—at least until He comes again. Jesus is doing this Himself. He says in Revelation, "Listen! I stand at the door and knock. If anyone hears My voice and opens the door, I will come in to him and have dinner with him, and he with Me" (3:20). Our task as disciples is to help Jesus knock. Jesus won't knock those doors down. That would be a violation of free will. We shouldn't expect Jesus to do this regardless of whether we help Him or not because Jesus uses us as His hands and feet. The church is the body of Christ (1 Cor. 12), the unit through which He works.

When a person closes the door of his or her heart to Jesus, why doesn't Christ just "knock the door down" and force His way in?

If we truly help Jesus knock, we will find doors opening. In Revelation, Jesus promised to set before the church of Philadelphia an "open door." He will also send open doors to the contemporary church that shows similar love and faithfulness. But most often we have to do the work of knocking.

In the book of Revelation, before what church did Jesus promise to set "an open door" (Rev. 3:8)? What does that say to the modern church?

Here are some suggested life changes to help you more effectively "knock" so that people will open the doors of their hearts to Jesus:

1. DEVELOP AND MAINTAIN A PRAYER LIST OF PEOPLE WHO NEED TO OPEN THEIR HEARTS TO JESUS. These should be people you know and to whom you might be able to witness (NOT some famous agnostic or world leader). Keep the list in your Bible to refer to during your devotional time or post it somewhere you will see it on a regular basis.

2. MEET SOMEONE WHO IS NOT A CHRISTIAN, AND LEARN THREE INTERESTING FACTS ABOUT THAT PERSON. Look especially for things you might have in common with this person. Don't try to witness to them right away, unless they voice an interest. For now you are seeking to develop a relationship that will eventually open doors. Pray for God's wisdom in developing this relationship.

life change lessons (cont'd)

3. HAVE A TRUSTED FRIEND HELP YOU EVALUATE HOW YOU SPEAK TO STRANGERS. This should be a person you can trust to be honest with you, while at the same time be loving and helpful. Have the person take note of the following: Does what you say show a genuine interest in others? Do you use a lot of negative and judgmental words? Is your tone harsh and standoffish or warm and inviting?

CARING TIME
Remain in groups of 6–8 people, in a horseshoe configuration.

Hand out the Prayer/Praise Report to the entire group. Ask each subgroup to pray for the empty chair. Pray specifically for God to guide you to someone to bring next week to fill that chair.

After a sufficient time of prayer in subgroups, close in a corporate prayer. Say, "Next week we will talk about: 'Teamtastic.' "

Remind participants of the daily Scripture readings and reflective questions found on page 152.

Caring Time (15-20 minutes)

Come together now for a time of sharing and prayer. Begin by listening to each other's dreams for the class or group by having each group member answer the following question:

"What doors would you like to see open for this group as we head on to other studies and think of new challenges?"

Pray for the dreams that people share. Then move on to praying for the concerns on the Prayer/Praise Report.

notes:

BIBLE STUDY NOTES

Reference Notes

Use these notes to gain further understanding of the text as you study on your own.

COLOSSIANS 4:2

Devote yourselves to prayer. See the example of the church in Acts 1:14; 2:42; and 6:4.
stay alert. An allusion to Matthew 26:41 and Luke 18:1. This call to vigilance and spiritual alertness became part of the apostles' teaching to Christians in general (Acts 20:31; 1 Cor. 16:13; 1 Thess. 5:6; 1 Pet. 5:8).

COLOSSIANS 4:3

the mystery of the Messiah. See 1:25-27.
in prison. Paul, imprisoned several times because Jewish opponents considered his missionary activity as subversive to their interests, probably wrote this letter while under the house arrest described in Acts 28.

COLOSSIANS 4:4

that I may reveal it as I am required to speak. In Ephesians 6:20, Paul asked for prayer that he might speak fearlessly. He knew that soon his case would come before the emperor.

COLOSSIANS 4:5

outsiders. By this Paul meant nonbelieving neighbors and associates.
making the most of the time. A similar passage in Ephesians 5:15 refers to the Christian's general conduct. In view here, however, is the special importance of being alert to God-given opportunities to bear witness to Christ in the course of daily life.

COLOSSIANS 4:6

seasoned with salt. Since salt was used to preserve food and prevent corruption, this metaphor has the same import as Paul's words in Ephesians 4:29. The Christian's witness is not to be argumentative or arrogant, but respectful and gracious (2 Tim. 2:23-26).

notes:

12

Session 13

Teamtastic!

Prepare for the Session

	READINGS	REFLECTIVE QUESTIONS
Monday	Colossians 4:7-11	Who has encouraged your heart recently? Have you thanked that person for what they have done?
Tuesday	Colossians 4:12-15	For whom, besides yourself and your immediate family, are you working hard? Are you helping others to "stand mature" in the Lord (v. 12)?
Wednesday	Colossians 4:16-18	Is there a ministry Christ has given you to which you need to pay more attention?
Thursday	John 15:12-15	When have you developed friendships while working with others for Christ? What do you need to do to strengthen these friendships?
Friday	Luke 22:28-30	When your friends go through hard times, are you there for them? How are you showing support to them?
Saturday	Philippians 1:3-6	What have you begun that you need to make sure to finish? What support will you need from others to do this?
Sunday	Acts 20:32-38	When have you had to say goodbye to Christian friends? What memories of them and your experiences together remain in your heart?

OUR GOALS FOR THIS SESSION ARE:

In groups of 6–8, gather people in a horseshoe configuration.

Make sure everyone has a name tag.

Take time to share information on class parties that are coming up as well as any relevant church events.

BIBLE STUDY
- to see what made the Christians who worked with Paul such an effective ministry team
- to consider ways to encourage one another in the faith
- to acknowledge the importance focusing on ministry goals has for effective team ministry

LIFE CHANGE
- to choose one leader in our church to encourage in some way each week
- to commit to praying daily for our pastor or pastoral team
- to obtain our church's mission statement and find one thing we can do to help make that mission happen

Icebreaker (10-15 minutes)

INTRODUCE THE ICEBREAKER ACTIVITY: The students have been given instructions in their books.

After the Icebreaker say something like, "Paul did not accomplish all that he accomplished alone. He was part of a team with many good people, some of whom we know today by name only. That's part of the reality of life. Teams are made up of more than the 'heroes' whose names get known to the world or sometimes to history. God honors every member of one of Christ's teams even if they are not known to others. In this session we will look at our need to be a part of a team like Paul's."

A Great Team! Go around the group on question 1 and let everyone share. Then go around again on questions 2 and 3, as time allows.

1. Looking back over your life, what is the greatest "team" experience that you've had?
   - ☐ a sports team in junior high or high school
   - ☐ a drama cast I was in during high school
   - ☐ a sports team I was on in college or as an adult
   - ☐ a drama cast I was in during college or as an adult
   - ☐ a project team at work
   - ☐ a ministry or mission team
   - ☐ a team that worked on a community project
   - ☐ other: ____________________

2. What do you enjoy the most about being part of a great team?
   - ☐ WINNING!
   - ☐ the camaraderie
   - ☐ all the attention I get from the crowd
   - ☐ doing something that makes a difference
   - ☐ feeling I can contribute and that I am needed
   - ☐ the satisfaction that comes from accomplishment
   - ☐ getting to know people better
   - ☐ other: ____________________

Hand out the Prayer/ Praise Report. A sample copy is at the back of this book. Have people write down prayer requests and praises. Then have the prayer coordinator collect the reports and make copies for use during the Caring Time.

Icebreaker (cont'd)

3. If you could assemble a team to work on one problem or area of need right now, what problem or need would you choose?

notes:

LEARNING FROM THE BIBLE

COLOSSIANS 4:7-18

Have a member of the class, selected ahead of time, read Colossians 4:7-18.

Bible Study (30-45 minutes)

The Scripture for this week:

7Tychicus, a loved brother, a faithful servant, and a fellow slave in the Lord, will tell you all the news about me. 8I have sent him to you for this very purpose, so that you may know how we are, and so that he may encourage your hearts. 9He is with Onesimus, a faithful and loved brother, who is one of you. They will tell you about everything here.

10Aristarchus, my fellow prisoner, greets you, as does Mark, Barnabas' cousin (concerning whom you have received instructions: if he comes to you, welcome him), 11and so does Jesus who is called Justus. These alone of the circumcision are my co-workers for the kingdom of God, and they have been a comfort to me. 12Epaphras, who is one of you, a slave of Christ Jesus, greets you. He is always contending for you in his prayers, so that you can stand mature and fully assured in everything God wills. 13For I testify about him that he works hard for you, for those in Laodicea, and for those in Hierapolis. 14Luke, the loved physician, and Demas greet you. 15Give my greetings to the brothers in Laodicea, and to Nympha and the church in her house. 16And when this letter has been read among you, have it read also in the church of the Laodiceans; and see that you also read the letter from Laodicea. 17And tell Archippus, "Pay attention to the ministry you have received in the Lord, so that you can accomplish it."

18This greeting is in my own hand—Paul. Remember my imprisonment. Grace be with you.

...about today's session (5 minutes)

Summarize these introductory remarks. Be sure to include the underlined information, which gives the answers to the student book questions (provided in the margin).

THE IMPORTANCE OF THE TEAM

America has been called the land of the "rugged individualist." Many people we revere have not been those who worked well with others. Instead, they have risen above the crowd to go their own way. One of our greatest heroes has been John Wayne. He always played the "my way or the highway" type of character. We have given more attention to the lone trailblazers like Kit Carson, Daniel Boone, and Davy Crockett than to the nameless pioneers who worked together along the trails to establish settlements. Sports teams with the "no-name defense" have been the exception, while we have pointed to stars like Michael Jordan, Barry Bonds, Shaquille O'Neal, or Peyton Manning, as if their play alone mattered.

How do you see the emphasis in our country on individualism affecting the work of the church?

Certainly people who act or perform alone can be important. But there comes a time when we have to acknowledge how important the team is. Teams that rely too much on stars seldom rise to championship level. That is especially true in the church. Some churches have hired pastors with impressive credentials thinking they would be the "star" that would send their ministry forward. In the end, however, most churches learn that a great deal of teamwork is required to succeed no matter who the senior pastor is.

What are two reasons why a "star" approach to ministry most often does not work?

The "star" approach most often does not work for several reasons. One is that the task at hand is usually bigger than any one person. Sports places natural limits on what any one person can do. A batter in baseball can only hit once every nine times. A star basketball player without skilled teammates gets double- or triple-teamed. A great defensive back in football often finds the other team running and throwing to the opposite side of the field so he cannot make plays. Then there is the fact that the other team has a star. In ministry, the task of bringing people to Christ and ministering to their needs in our post-modern world is more complicated than ever. So many interests and perspectives compete for the attention of the people–from movies, music, and television to Eastern religions and New Age philosophy to computer games and the Internet. Overcoming all of these challenges is more than one person can handle.

What are some factors that make ministering in today's world complicated?

Another reason the "star" approach does not work is that it prevents others from feeling needed and "owning" the challenge before them. The star will solve the problem. The star will get the glory. The other team members feel unnecessary.

In today's text we discover that Paul was not a lone star who did it all. He acknowledged his team. In so doing he showed the importance of the team for what we do in ministry. Today we will be looking at that importance.

Remain in groups of 6–8 people, in a horseshoe configuration.

In this small-group session, students will be responding to the following questions that will help them share their stories in terms of the teamwork expressed in Colossians 4:7-18.

Have the students explore these questions together.

Identifying with the Story (5-7 minutes)

1. What friends do you have who fill the same functions as the following people did for Paul or for the Christians at Colossae?
   - Tychicus—the communicator, the one who keeps you informed about old friends away from you ________
   - Aristarchus—the "fellow prisoner," the one who has been through a lot with you ________
   - Onesimus & Epaphras—the "kindred spirits," the ones who are closest to you ________ & ________
   - Epaphras—the prayer warrior, the one who has "always contended for you" in his or her prayers ________
   - Mark & Justus—the comforters, the ones who have done the most to lift you when you were down ________ & ________
2. What would you tell someone who hasn't seen you for a while about your life that might encourage their heart?
3. What difficulty in your life would you like people to remember right now, as Paul wanted people to remember his imprisonment?

notes:

today's session (15-20 minutes)

Share with your class the following information which you may modify according to your own perspectives and teaching needs. The answers to the student book questions (provided in the margin) are underlined.

Paul put together a great team. They started strong churches throughout Europe and Asia, including Pisidian Antioch, Lystra, Iconium, Derbe, Philippi, Thessalonica, Berea, Corinth, and Ephesus. Even the church at Colossae, though not started by Paul himself, was started by one of his team members. Because of their teamwork, the gospel of Jesus Christ grew from being a tiny movement in Israel to being a religion spread throughout the Roman world.

When you have a great team, it is always a good idea to learn from it and discover what made it a great team. In basketball or football you might want to ask what style of defense they are using or what they do to mask offensive plays. In baseball you might do a statistical analysis of when they tend to steal, hit-and-run, or bunt, or you may look at how strong they are up the middle defensively.

What are four factors that made the team Paul assembled a great ministerial team?

In the same way we need to discover what made Paul's team such a good team. Looking at this week's passage we can find four contributing factors—mutual encouragement, prayer, hard work, and keeping focused on the goal.

Mutual Encouragement

Paul told the Colossians that he had sent Tychicus to them "so that you may know how we are, and so that he may encourage your hearts" (v. 8). This was a common practice with Paul. When he could not go to a church where he had a relationship with the members, he sent someone else. He sent Timothy when he was worried about the well-being of the Christians at Thessalonica (1 Thess. 3:1-5); to Corinth he sent Titus and an unnamed Christian brother (2 Cor. 8:16-18); to Philippi he sent Timothy (Phil. 2: 19-24); and to Ephesus he once more sent Tychicus (Eph.. 6:21-22). In return, churches sometimes sent people to encourage and assist Paul. Philippi sent Epaphroditus for that purpose (Phil. 2:25-30), and a delegation of Christians came to encourage and assist Paul when he arrived at Rome (Acts 28:15). Such actions were in accord with Paul's instructions to the Thessalonians to "encourage one another and build each other up as you are already doing" (1 Thess. 5:11). It's important to note that this encouragement was not a one-way thing. Paul both gave it and received it. That's what it means to be part of a team—all give and all receive.

Who were some people Paul sent to the churches to encourage them?

This encouragement was especially important at this time since the believers faced so many difficulties. Paul himself was in prison at the time he wrote this letter to the Colossians (v. 18). During the course of his ministry he went through everything from being shipwrecked to being persecuted, flogged, and even stoned by his opponents (for a more complete list of his hardships see 2 Cor. 11:23-29).

Why was mutual encouragement so important in Paul's time?

today's session (cont'd)

The Christians to whom Paul was writing were already being thrown out of the synagogues, and those in Rome would soon face Nero's bloody persecution. In the midst of such things if Christians didn't pull together, they would pull apart.

We also live in difficult times. In many places where we live and work the one truly dedicated to Christ represents a distinct minority. We need mutual encouragement to stand up for ethical business practices, courteous treatment of co-workers (as opposed to racism, manipulation, and harassment), and respectful language.

Prayer

Last week we talked of the importance of prayer in opening doors to ministry. That is certainly an important part of a team approach to ministry. Even when we cannot be part of a work directly, we can always be part of it through prayer. But when you are part of a team, prayer for each other's personal needs is vital. Here Epaphras was exemplary as Paul told the Colossians, "He is always contending for you in his prayers, so that you can stand mature and fully assured in everything God wills" (v. 12). The Greek word translated "contending for you" was often used in relation to track and field contests. In various versions it is translated "laboring fervently in prayer" (KJV), "wrestling in prayer" (NIV), and "prays hard" (NEB). In any case, this is not light, casual prayer! It may imply contending against evil spiritual forces.

Praying in the spirit of Epaphras means realizing that the other members of our team are contending against some pretty heavy spiritual issues and that they need our help in prayer. Some battle addictions. Some have strained marriages. Some are still dealing with personal traumas from their childhood. And yet none of these are too big for a team of people "contending for" each other in prayer. As James reminds us, "The intense prayer of the righteous is very powerful" (5:16).

Hard Work

Our team involvement cannot end with prayer—we must also work hard. Besides praying hard, Epaphras also worked hard for the Colossians (v. 13). The whole team had to work hard. They traveled back and forth over hundreds of miles of roads. Setting up a daily camp and providing food for the team would be time-consuming. Some, like Paul, sought to maintain a trade at the same time they were preaching and teaching (Acts 18:2-3). But that is just the physical work. They also faced hard emotional work—contending with opposition, dealing with governing authorities suspicious of their work.

What are some examples of the "hard work" that people like Epaphras had to do as part of Paul's team?

and doing all that is required to establish trusting relationships with converts and potential converts.

Hard work is also required for the church to thrive today. All sorts of people want to sell churches easy answers—get the right pastor, buy this successful program, read these books. But in the end it always takes people who are willing to give of their time to visit or call or share their faith or pick up people to bring them to church. Churches or ministry teams who want to avoid having to put in time or work will not get far, no matter what program they buy.

Focusing on the Goal

Finally, a team must always keep its eye on its goal. A successful pro football team shoots for the Super Bowl. A winning baseball team sets its sights on winning the World Series. In basketball you go for nothing less than the NBA title. Paul always kept his eye on his goal. He wrote in Philippians 3:13-14: "But one thing I do: forgetting what is behind and reaching forward to what is ahead, I pursue as my goal the prize promised by God's heavenly call in Christ Jesus." This focus on his goal drove Paul, and he expected the same from the people with whom he worked. He wanted the Colossians to tell Archippus, "Pay attention to the ministry you have received in the Lord, so that you can accomplish it" (v. 17). We don't know specifically what this ministry was, but Paul wanted him to keep focused on it because a loss of focus can affect the whole team.

What did Paul see as his own life goal, as reported in Philippians?

Churches and ministry teams must be focused on their goal today as well. An old joke tells of Jesus coming back to earth and visiting a church. When the church leaders found out, they went to the Senior Pastor and asked, "What should we do?" All the Senior Pastor could say was, "I don't know, but look busy!" Too many churches just try to look busy, but what is their goal? What is the unique mission God has given them? It is a focus on the goal that makes a winning team.

notes:

Remain in groups of 6–8 people, in a horseshoe configuration.

In this small-group session, students will be applying the lessons of the text to their own lives through the following questions.

The students were asked (in the student book) to choose an answer for each question and explain why.

Learning from the Story (5-7 minutes)

1. What would you say is the best way for Christians to "encourage each other's hearts"?

   ☐ affirming the good things that I see them doing
   ☐ telling what I have seen God doing in my life
   ☐ listening to them
   ☐ reminding them of the promises of God
   ☐ other: ____________________

2. What needs to happen for members of this group to more effectively "contend for each other in prayer"?

3. What is the main thing that diverts your attention from focusing on your ministry? When this happens, what can members of this class do to help you regain your focus?

notes:

Share with the class the following thoughts on how the lessons of this text might be applied today. The answers to the student book questions (provided in the margin) are underlined unless the question requires a personal answer.

life change lessons (5-7 minutes)

What do you do if your team isn't winning? If it's a sports team, you change the coach, or you trade for (or purchase) new players. Even then these tactics fail at least as often as they succeed. Sometimes the difference between a losing season and a winning one is not so easily defined. Over the course of several years, at the change of the millennium, the Seattle Mariners baseball team traded away stars Ken Griffey Jr., Randy Johnson, and Alex Rodriguez. The year after the last one left, many thought the Mariners would be in a "rebuilding" year; but they ended up winning more games in the regular season than any other team in baseball history. The reason seems to have been a well-balanced club with team chemistry. Perhaps that is an important key to building winning teams in ministry as well. We all have to contribute, and we have to bond together as a unit.

In order to build a "winning team," what two things must we do?

Some struggling churches try the approach of sports teams. They start by firing the coach. At one point the average stay of a pastor at a church in America was under three years. Others try to lure "star" members from other churches to come join theirs. Not only is this approach unethical and counter to what it means to be the body of Christ, but it doesn't work. A winning team has to *be* a team, not a few leaders with a bunch of spectators.

So what life changes does this suggest for individual Christians? We cannot make a "team" by ourselves. But we can do some things that will make us more effective team members and make it a little easier for others to work with us in a team situation.

In what four ways can we encourage one another?

1. CHOOSE ONE LEADER IN YOUR CHURCH TO ENCOURAGE IN SOME WAY EACH WEEK. This can be done by affirming something they did, by reminding them of the promises of God in Scripture, or by voicing your belief in them as a person. It should also include praying for them.

2. COMMIT TO PRAYING DAILY FOR YOUR PASTOR OR PASTORAL TEAM. Periodically go to your pastor or pastors and find out what matters they especially need prayer for, both personally and as pastor. Assure each pastor of your prayer for them.

3. OBTAIN YOUR CHURCH'S MISSION STATEMENT AND FIND ONE THING YOU CAN DO TO HELP MAKE THAT MISSION HAPPEN. The point here is not to become busier but to work more effectively for your church's mission. There may be some involvements you will want to drop because they don't really contribute to the church's mission. Find a way to get involved in something that *does* contribute to this mission.

CARING TIME
Remain in groups of 6–8 people, in a horseshoe configuration.

Hand out the Prayer/ Praise Report to the entire group. Be sure to allow enough time for the evaluation. If your group is going to continue, also allow time to discuss the covenant on the following pages. Close with a corporate prayer.

Caring Time (15-20 minutes)

Pray for the concerns listed on the Prayer/Praise Report, then continue with the evaluation and covenant.

1. Take some time to evaluate the life of your group by using the statements below. Read the first sentence out loud and ask everyone to explain where they would put a dot between the two extremes. When you are finished, go back and give your group an overall grade in the categories of Group Building, Bible Study, and Mission.

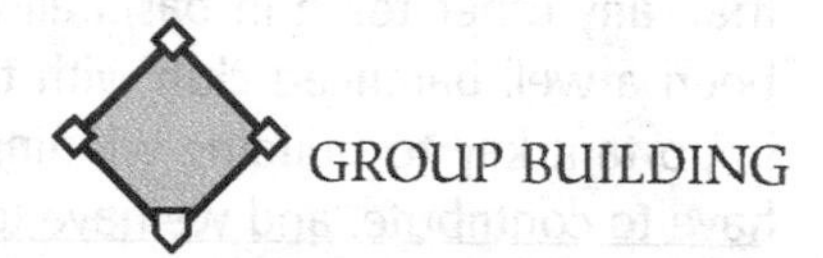

On celebrating life and having fun together, we were more like a ...
wet blanket ································ **hot tub**

On becoming a caring community, we were more like a ...
prickly porcupine ································ **cuddly teddy bear**

On sharing our spiritual stories, we were more like a ...
shallow pond ································ **spring-fed lake**

On digging into Scripture, we were more like a ...
slow-moving snail ································ **voracious anteater**

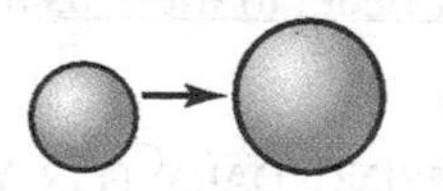

On inviting new people into our group, we were more like a ...
barbed-wire fence ································ **wide-open door**

On stretching our vision for mission, we were more like an ...
ostrich ································ **eagle**

2. What are some specific areas in which you have grown in this course?
   - ☐ being more open to the Holy Spirit's guidance
   - ☐ finding new ways to minister to other's needs

- ☐ handling conflict situations in the church with love and wisdom
- ☐ sharing faith and fellowship with other cultures
- ☐ understanding the power of prayer
- ☐ slowing down and letting the Holy Spirit guide me
- ☐ following ethical business practices
- ☐ other:______________________________

A covenant is a promise made to another in the presence of God. Its purpose is to indicate your intention to make yourselves available to one another for the fulfillment of the purposes you share in common. If your group is going to continue, in a spirit of prayer work your way through the following sentences, trying to reach an agreement on each statement pertaining to your ongoing life together. Write out your covenant like a contract, stating your purpose, goals, and the ground rules for your group.

1. The purpose of our group will be:

2. Our goals will be:

3. We will meet on ________________ (day of week).
4. We will meet for _____weeks, after which we will decide if we wish to continue as a group.
5. We will meet from _______ to _______ and we will strive to start on time and end on time.
6. We will meet at ____________________ (place) or we will rotate from house to house.
7. We will agree to the following ground rules for our group (check):
   - ☐ PRIORITY: While you are in this course of study, you give the group meetings priority.
   - ☐ PARTICIPATION: Everyone is encouraged to participate and no one dominates.
   - ☐ RESPECT: Everyone has the right to his or her own opinion, and all questions are encouraged and respected.

13

Caring Time (cont'd)

- ▢ CONFIDENTIALITY: Anything said in the meeting is never repeated outside the meeting.
- ▢ LIFE CHANGE: We will regularly assess our own life change goals and encourage one another in our pursuit of Christlikeness.
- ▢ EMPTY CHAIR: The group stays open to reaching new people at every meeting.
- ▢ CARE and SUPPORT: Permission is given to call upon each other at any time especially in times of crisis. The group will provide care for every member.
- ▢ ACCOUNTABILITY: We agree to let the members of the group hold us accountable to the commitments which each of us make in whatever loving ways we decide upon.
- ▢ MISSION: We will do everything in our power to start a new group.
- ▢ MINISTRY: The group will encourage one another to volunteer and serve in a ministry, and to support missions by giving financially and/or personally serving.

BIBLE STUDY NOTES

Reference Notes

Use these notes to gain further understanding of the text as you study on your own.

COLOSSIANS 4:7

Tychicus. Tychicus was a traveling companion of Paul in Acts 20:4.

COLOSSIANS 4:9

Onesimus. The converted slave was the subject of the letter to Philemon.
one of you. A fellow Colossian.

COLOSSIANS 4:10

Aristarchus. Another person mentioned in Acts 20:4 as traveling with Paul.
Mark, Barnabas' cousin. Barnabas and Paul had had a "parting of the ways" over whether Mark should be included on their second missionary journey after he had deserted them on the first journey (Acts 13:13; 15:36-41). This passage shows that there was a rapprochement between Mark and Paul. Paul lists him as one of his few Jewish co-workers and as one who had been a "comfort" to him.

COLOSSIANS 4:11

Jesus who is called Justus. Jesus was a rather common name of the time. Nothing is really known of this person other than what is written here.

COLOSSIANS 4:12

Epaphras. A native Colossian who established the church there and throughout the Lycus valley (1:7; Philem. 23). Paul's commendation here and in 1:7 substantiates his claim that the church had already heard the whole gospel.
a slave of Christ Jesus. Paul used this phrase elsewhere to describe himself (Rom. 1:1; Phil. 1:1). In so doing he both identified with and exalted the low estate of actual slaves in his call to them to render service as to the Lord (3:24). This further commendation of Epaphras would help assure the Colossians that he had indeed passed along the gospel to them.
always contending for you in his prayers. One dimension of devotion to prayer (4:2) is the realization that it is an encounter not only with God but against spiritual forces that seek to hinder God's work (Eph. 6:12). This was especially needed as the Colossians faced the challenge of the false teachers.
fully assured. Another "fullness" word to encourage the Colossian believers that in Christ they had all God has to bestow on people.

COLOSSIANS 4:13

Laodicea. A city just a few miles from Colossae, near the Lycus River.
Hierapolis. A city about twelve miles northwest of Colossae and six miles north of Laodicea.

COLOSSIANS 4:14

Luke, the loved physician. This reference reveals Luke's profession. The various "we" passages in the book of Acts (16:10-17; 20:5–21:18; 27:1–28:16) indicate that Luke accompanied Paul at several points in his missionary work.

COLOSSIANS 4:15

Nympha and the church in her house. The Laodicean church, or at least part of it, followed the custom of other early churches in meeting in the homes of members who could accommodate them. Philemon's home was the site of the congregation in Colossae (Philem. 1-2).

COLOSSIANS 4:16

The epistles were written to address specific problems and concerns of the various churches to which they were written. They were meant to be read at gatherings of the church.
the letter from Laodicea. Some have thought that this might be what is now our letter to the Ephesians since no specific destination is mentioned in that letter. It is more likely that this is a lost letter, like the one Paul refers to in 2 Corinthians 2:4,9.

COLOSSIANS 4:17

Archippus. Philemon 2 calls him a "fellow soldier." Since he is the only Colossian specifically addressed in the letter, he may have been a leading elder in the church.

COLOSSIANS 4:18

This greeting is in my own hand—Paul. Typically, others actually wrote Paul's letters at his dictation (Rom. 16:22) while he penned the final greeting as a mark of the letter's genuineness (1 Cor. 16:21; Gen. 6:11; 2 Thess. 3:17; Philem. 19). Second Thessalonians 2:2 hints at the possibility that forged letters had been circulated in Paul's name.
Grace be with you. Paul's common greeting sums up the essence of his message to this church—that they are saved completely through the gracious work of Jesus Christ on their behalf.

Name	Phone No.

Pray and Praise Pages

Pray for ...

Praise God for ...